YELP HELP

D1057235

YELP HELP

How to Write Great
Online Restaurant Reviews

HANNA RASKIN

Copyright © 2013 Hanna Raskin
All Rights Reserved

The author is an independent food critic and is not affiliated
with Yelp. The contents and opinions in this book belong to
the author alone and should not be imputed to anyone else.
This book is not supported or endorsed by Yelp or any other
online reviewing website.

ISBN 978-1-49-095554-4 (paper)
Version 1.0.2 (10 July 2013)

Cover by CL Smith
Book design by Matthew Amster-Burton

Table of Contents

Introduction

PROFESSIONAL FOOD CRITICS ARE FOND of pointing out that one opinion can't sink a restaurant: If a restaurant's doing everything right, a published gripe about the amount of salt in the osso buco or a chipped porcelain plate won't put it out of business.

To cite one example from my reviewing career, I'm no fan of periodically splaying open the doors of a barbecue pit to show prospective eaters the meat which awaits them, since that kind of showmanship disrupts the ancient duet of heat and animal flesh. But as I'm constantly reminding the aggrieved pitmaster who tends to e-mail me after he's been out drinking, my saying so in print doesn't doom a business plan built around the practice. Maybe folks are fools for smoked-meat theater. Or maybe they only care about coleslaw quality. Either way, the best I can hope to do is start a conversation about tradition, technology, and time.

As a food critic, I've had the good fortune to work at alternative newsweeklies in Asheville, N.C., Dallas, and Seattle, jobs which allowed me to sample every slaw dog in three southern Appalachian counties; master the intricacies of cheese enchiladas; and learn how to distinguish a Totten Inlet oyster from a Naked Roy oyster. I figure the thousands of hours I've spent poking around restaurants qualifies me to give folks sound advice about which edible visions are worth supporting.

Yet much as I might wish it was otherwise when I encounter a strip-mall restaurant run by a native Hungarian who stays up until 4 a.m. tussling with swine meat and sausage casings, we paid reviewers have very little say in whether a restaurant thrives or fails. Perhaps there was an era when an Anton Ego's tsk-tsking could lead directly to an "out of business" sign. But nowadays, the power to determine a restaurant's future rests almost entirely with civilian eaters.

That's not just the industry's impression: Plenty of respected academics have argued that Yelp reviews correlate precisely with a restaurant's sales. In 2011, a Harvard Business School researcher who'd crunched six years' worth of data from Seattle reported that restaurants increase their revenue by 5 to 9 percent for each additional Yelp star. And a pair of UC Berkeley economists in 2012 announced that an extra half-star is all it takes for a restaurant to have a 30 to 49 percent better chance of selling out its tables on any given evening. What's written on sites such as Yelp, TripAdvisor, and Urbanspoon matters enormously to restaurant owners whose life savings are tied up in their projects; chefs whose reputations ride on their artistry; local farmers who need dependable outlets for their beets and kale; and servers who struggle to pay the rent when they lose a shift or two.

The reason so many restaurateurs hate online reviewing

sites is that citizen critics often wield their power with all the grace of an elephant with a javelin. They hold restaurants accountable for circumstances beyond their control (believe me, any restaurant owner who's bothered to install a patio also wishes it hadn't rained the day you visited). They prattle on about amenities which are purely tangential to the restaurant experience, such as the color of the bussers' shirts, and scold the chef for daring to deviate from Granny's recipe for green-chile casserole.

To be fair, many of the most egregious online reviews are written by vindictive diners who'd rather flaunt their own culinary expertise or pen a mini-memoir than help fellow diners. But even if Yelp was wiped clean of grudges and narcissism, I'd wager most restaurateurs would keep bad-mouthing the site. That's because, aside from concerns about whether Yelp plays fair – it took years for the site to defeat a class action suit brought by business owners who claimed positive write-ups vanished when they refused to buy advertising – far too many reviews come off as clueless.

I'm certain the vast majority of online reviewers are well-meaning. But as someone who relies on sites such as Yelp for restaurant leads, I'm sympathetic to complaints about the bad writing, questionable food knowledge, and misplaced petulance that have become the hallmarks of amateur food reviewing. (If you haven't yet watched the "Real Actors Read Yelp Reviews" YouTube series, I'll wait.)

The democratization of culinary culture is hugely exciting: I love the idea that a guy who will never land a food-writing job because he refuses to eat anything but ramen, or because he doesn't want to give up his day gig laying pipe, or because nobody's hiring food writers anymore, can steer me to the best damn bowl of noodles in Butte, Montana. But all of us – restaurant owners, restaurant workers, and restaurant-goers – would be better off if the overall quality of online reviews was a notch higher.

And if the prospect of elevated food discourse isn't reason enough to invest more time in producing thoughtful, engaging reviews, sites such as Yelp sweeten the pot with material rewards: A reviewer who earns elite status on Yelp is eligible to attend private parties and collect Yelp-branded gifts. More crucially, elite Yelpers are granted an online badge which signals to readers that they know their stuff. According to Yelp, "Elite-worthiness is based on a number of things, including well-written reviews." If you write great reviews, elite status will surely follow.

The problem is, reviewing isn't like singing or dancing. Nobody's born with the ability to do it well. It's a skill, just like welding or making a rabbit disappear. Some people have more of a knack for it than others, but mastery of restaurant criticism really hinges on learning a set of fundamentals and practicing them. The same techniques apply whether you're reviewing an Eric Ripert restaurant in New York City or a Filipino lunch counter at the end of your block.

I know that doesn't sound as sexy as the Sauternes and foie gras that many eaters envision when they hear the words "restaurant review." But if you participate in an online restaurant-reviewing community because you want to share the joys and frustrations of your search for a memorable meal – and benefit from your fellow diners' triumphant quests for the same – you know this avocation involves more than luxury and snark. It takes a measure of seriousness and know-how, which is what this book will give you. By sticking to the principles outlined here, you'll be able to write reviews which contribute to our collective culinary conversation and enrich your readers' dining adventures. And if other online reviewers are inspired to hold themselves to your high standards, you'll soon be eating better too.

In the pages ahead, you'll learn the story of the world's first restaurant reviewer; why certain restaurants don't take reservations; how to figure out who's responsible when your food shows up cold; and what description you should never, ever leave out of an online review. Perhaps you're already anxious to get typing. But just as it's impossible to cook a great meal without first learning to taste, reading necessarily comes before writing. Let's have some fun.

CHAPTER 1

Demystifying the Restaurant

THERE'S A REASON MIDDLE SCHOOLS mount productions of *Our Town* instead of the latest Cirque du Soleil extravaganza: The magic of the latter is contingent upon elaborate obfuscation devices which make it seem as though the performers are really flying unassisted and dissolving into puffs of smoke. Watching the algebra teacher hoist a chubby kid on a thick black wire doesn't have the same effect.

Special effects dazzle because the audience isn't in on the tricks. But the technicians charged with pulling off the spectacle have to understand how every mechanism works so they can fix them when they break. Restaurant reviewers are in a similar position: In order to fairly and accurately assess the problems they confront in a dining room, they need to have a tight grasp on restaurant operations. A restaurant's refusal to accommodate a request for a no-egg, no-dairy, no-wheat dinner, for instance, might make more sense to a guest who knows something about pantry inventories and kitchen prep.

Admittedly, some of the romance of eating out is dimmed when restaurant secrets are revealed; managers and maître d's go to great lengths to keep the clockwork hidden. But a review meal isn't about surrendering to fantasy. It's an opportunity to scrutinize a restaurant, to glean details which will help other eaters decide whether or not they want to patronize the place. Remember, if the meal's exceptional, you can always return while off-duty.

Familiarity with restaurant operations can also help make dining out a more comfortable and enjoyable experience. If you're a longtime restaurant-goer, you're probably at ease with wine lists and cheese carts. Perhaps, though, you've shared a restaurant table with friends who are skittish about talking to servers or tense up when forced to determine the tip. Or maybe you've been seated alongside a nervous couple intent on replicating the rhythms of dinner at home, ordering two of the same entrées and water to drink.

I'm always surprised by how many smart, competent adults get sweaty at the thought of eating a fancy meal in a restaurant. Their anxieties probably reflect economic realities, which prevent most hourly-wage workers from eating out at the pace required to become comfortable with the quirks of fine dining, but they're also partly the fault of sneering servers and the current generation of self-important chefs, who are more interested in the composition of their plates than the desires of their customers. Those types aren't omnipresent, by any stretch: I eat out six or seven nights a week, and if I meet two or three jerks over the course of a month, I consider it a bad run. (Restaurant service standards are intensely local, so you might have better or worse luck based on your home ZIP code.) But it only takes one wannabe Soup Nazi to persuade an infrequent restaurant-goer that every move is a po-

tential breach of etiquette. Figuring out how restaurants actu-
ally work is the best way to overcome the worry that spoils too
many outstanding meals.

Of course, there's no single, success-guaranteed template
for a restaurant. Many entrepreneurs learn this the hard way,
when they religiously follow every bullet point in a how-to
guide and then watch their restaurants nosedive into obliv-
ion. Online restaurant-review sites give a good sense of the
industry's breadth: If you scroll through the newest posts,
you're likely to come across food trucks, counter-service
burger joints, all-night diners, brewpubs, Chinese takeout
specialists, steakhouses, and small-plate bistros – and those
are just the most obvious conceptual differences. There are
big restaurants and small restaurants; old restaurants and
new restaurants; independently owned restaurants and
restaurants run by giant corporations. Yet there are enough
commonalities among all the different kinds of restaurants
that understanding how just one subspecies works will put
you in fine stead.

•

For our purposes, let's explore what most Americans would
consider a "regular sit-down restaurant." Our imaginary 100-
seat restaurant has a full bar and slightly edgy art on the walls,
but it's popular with families because there's a children's
menu with chicken fingers. The youngsters tend to clear out
by 8 p.m., when date traffic picks up: It's not uncommon for
a couple here to split a goat-cheese flatbread before moving
on to their Caesar salads and $18 entrées. If he's having the
seared tuna and she's having the pesto penne primavera, they
might order a bottle of California Chardonnay; if their dishes
don't overlap, they might ask for two different microbrews.

The restaurant – we'll call it The Standard – doesn't offer free bread, but servers bring crisp, slender breadsticks with a signature whipped garlic dip to every table.

You know this restaurant, right? You've doubtless seen restaurants like it in neighborhoods, malls, and hotels across the country. Still, no matter how many times you've dined at similar restaurants, The Standard looks different to the people who work there. To get a better handle on what's happening behind the scenes, let's check in with the restaurant's staffers. Then, after we've met the cast, we'll run through what happens when a party of two arrives for dinner.

•

Just as every football team has an offensive line and a defensive line, every restaurant crew is split in two: front-of-the-house and back-of-the-house (abbreviated as FOH and BOH in help-wanted ads and industry tweets). As the name suggests, front-of-the-house encompasses all the employees who interact with guests, such as hostess, bartender, sommelier, and server. Back-of-the-house refers to cooking and cleaning.

Since back-of-the-house tasks are mostly executed out of public sight – although that's less true in the age of open kitchens – BOH staffers are apt to be rougher than their comrades on the floor, but it's the rare restaurant employee who isn't well-versed in drinking and cursing. While there are far more women involved in the industry today, the food-and-beverage ethos is still staunchly macho, even in restaurants where dainty soufflés are prepared tableside and coffee is served with demitasse spoons.

In many pocket-sized restaurants run by couples, one partner takes care of the FOH and one partner tends to BOH duties. On the other end of the spectrum, a typical Cheese-cake Factory may put as many as 100 BOH staffers on its schedule. At The Standard, there are a dozen employees in the following BOH roles:

HEAD CHEF

The head chef is responsible for all the food served in the restaurant. He or she creates the menu in accordance with food costs, trends, and the owner's vision. At countless small restaurants, the chef is the owner. But the owner may also be a group of investors or a chef who's given up the rigors of daily cooking for moguldom: If you're dining at one of the many restaurants associated with a celebrity, your meal was probably dreamed up by the head chef, not the executive chef whose name you know. That doesn't mean the food quality is diminished, but it's worth knowing that the premium you pay to dine at a James Beard Foundation–blessed restaurant doesn't guarantee a glimpse of the chef you've seen on TV.

In addition to supervising inventories and writing recipes, the head chef is also in charge of the kitchen staff. Since lots of cooks like to get rowdy (see above), BOH turnover is a constant in all but the finest restaurants. In larger restaurants, the head chef may delegate management responsibilities to a chef de cuisine, kitchen manager, or sous chef, but it's not unusual for a head chef in a restaurant the size of The Standard to deal with ingredient order forms and scheduling requests.

Incidentally, the accepted honorific for the head chef is "chef." If the head chef approaches your table to ask after your meal, it's perfectly appropriate to end your conversation with "Thank you, chef," just as the cooks in the kitchen do. If dinner was lousy and you have something less gracious to say, you can omit the "chef" bit.

SOUS CHEF (or CHEF DE CUISINE)

Essentially the restaurant's deputy commander, the sous chef runs the kitchen. He or she leads the BOH team in the head chef's absence and makes sure its members are doing what's expected of them. Depending on the restaurant, the sous chef may also contribute ideas for dishes.

PASTRY CHEF

A growing number of restaurants are relying on their head chefs to think up sweets as well as savories, but oldfangled high-end restaurants and restaurants looking to elevate their dessert programs still keep bakers on their payrolls. In addition to fooling around with dried figs and fondant, the pastry chef usually doubles as the in-house bread baker, which is why his or her hours are often at odds with every other kitchen schedule. The pastry chef may arrive at the restaurant before dawn and clock out by early afternoon, leaving butter rolls in the oven and hand-churned rhubarb-fennel ice cream in the walk-in freezer.

PREP COOK

Culinary-school grads and self-taught cooks who end up working for restaurants are generally drawn into the industry by its perpetual craziness and bustle; their even-keeled counterparts tend to gravitate toward catering companies and hospital cafeterias. Prep cooks, though, see a significantly more sedate side of the restaurant business, since they typically work while the restaurant's closed. As the name suggests, prep cooks specialize in do-ahead work: They might spend their afternoons shucking dozens of ears of corn for a nightly vegetable special, dicing chicken for the salad station, or debearding mussels for gallons of bouillabaisse.

Prep cooks nearly always head home before the restaurant

opens, although if staff meal (also known as "family meal") is dished out before service, they might stick around to eat first. Family meal isn't offered at every restaurant: Many restaurants instead allow workers to order discounted food off the menu before or after their shifts. But The Standard's honchos like the concept because it's a daily chance to use up leftovers, experiment with new recipes, and gather staffers for group announcements. Plus, the practice helps ensure a well-fed crew, which is an important consideration when diners are still adding their names to the wait list at 10 p.m., five hours after the start of service.

LINE COOK

Most of the cooks you observe cooking your meal are line cooks. These are the men and women – often tattooed, always branded with burn marks – who prepare the dishes listed on the menu.

Line cooks are assigned to various stations organized by preparation technique. Traditional restaurant kitchens have areas dedicated to saucing, grilling, frying, and roasting, but a modern restaurant may simply divide its kitchen into hot and cold stations. Eggplant parmigiana comes from the former, eggplant hummus comes from the latter. Stations are notorious for working at different speeds, which is why you may see your fried chicken languish under a heat lamp while the cold station guy's still bumbling around the pantry, trying to find the croutons for your friend's salad.

EXPEDITER

In many restaurants, the sous chef functions as the expediter, or expo, since the job offers the best vantage point from which to keep track of the kitchen. The expo stands on the non-cooking side of the service window or pass (folks who haven't worked in restaurants would likely call it a counter or shelf), which is where completed dishes are placed to await pickup. He or she makes sure every dish is arranged correctly, without any missing garnishes or stray sauce marks on its rim, and matches dishes to order tickets so a server doesn't grab a meatloaf intended for one table and deliver it to another.

A sizable majority of restaurants now use point-of-sale (POS) computer systems, so a small printer spits out order tickets; the expo then relays their content to the line cooks, using abbreviations whenever possible. When your carefully thought-out order for "the New York strip, cooked until there's just a hint of pink, perhaps accompanied by a side of mashed potatoes" reaches the kitchen, it's read as "strip, mid-well, mash." And if you hear an expo bark "six shrimp all day," that means there are active tickets showing that six people in the entire restaurant have placed orders for the sriracha shrimp with coconut rice.

DISHWASHER

While the dishwasher's job is fairly straightforward, many restaurant pros believe it's the most important job in the kitchen, because even the most talented chef can't prepare food for public consumption in dirty pots and pans. Nearly every highfalutin chef and floor manager has done time in the dish pit, since the job can't go undone just because somebody calls in sick. Although nearly every restaurant is equipped with a commercial dish machine, the contraption is built for speed, not convenience. It still takes a human to rinse the thousands of plates, utensils, and kitchen tools that a restaurant dirties over the course of an evening, and to dry them when the mechanical cleaning cycle is complete.

Dishwashing is hard, underpaid work, which is why it's a

job often left to workers with the least resources. According to a 2008 study from the Pew Hispanic Center, nearly one in three dishwashers in the U.S. is an undocumented immigrant. Although other back-of-the-house positions appeal to a slightly more diverse workforce, 20 percent of the nation's cooking jobs are held by undocumented immigrants. As a result, Spanish is the first language of kitchens turning out everything from high-end steaks to Japanese noodles.

·

Of course, cooks and dishwashers aren't unique to restaurants: Mining camps and nursing homes employ cooks and dishwashers too. The difference between those establishments and restaurants such as The Standard is service, which is the realm of the front-of-the-house staffers. Let's say hello, shall we?

MANAGER
During the day, a manager might count vodka bottles, meet with a magazine's advertising representative, evaluate requests for charitable donations, install a bathroom soap dispenser, print specials sheets, and order new server aprons. But once service starts, the manager's primary responsibility is overseeing restaurant operations. He or she may be called upon to expedite food when the kitchen's slammed or nip a blossoming fight between the hostess and the bartender. In most restaurants, the manager is forever adjusting checks to reflect guests' coupons and correct server errors (some point-of-sale systems make it surprisingly easy to inadvertently order 200 grilled cheese sandwiches when the customer wanted only two).

Above all else, the manager is charged with making sure

guests are happy. Even if the manager doesn't function as a traditional maître d', researching your cocktail preferences ahead of your arrival and arranging for your table to be set with your favorite flowers, he or she is expected to stay abreast of what's happening in the dining room. The best managers circulate throughout the restaurant, proactively apologizing to customers whose entrées are slow to arrive and sending free drinks to the unfortunate table which took the brunt of a busser's water-pitcher bobble.

While there are no strict rules regarding restaurant flubs and consolation prizes – an overcooked steak isn't necessarily good for a gift certificate, nor should a diner made to wait past his reservation time automatically look for a comped cheesecake slice – it's understood throughout the restaurant industry that a manager's job is to at least try to resolve complaints to the customer's satisfaction. Unfortunately, many customers are reluctant to complain. If anything is interfering with your enjoyment, from a too-salty soup to a too-cold room, it's perfectly legitimate to bring the problem to the manager's attention; just remember you're entitled to a solution, not a freebie.

BARTENDER

Bartending has changed drastically in recent years as cocktail culture has grown increasingly sophisticated. Knowing how to mix a highball and pull a pint of beer is far from a sufficient skill set in an age when consumers are familiar with six different kinds of vermouth.

But too many bartenders (the term "mixologist" is used almost exclusively by publicity flacks) have lately become overly engrossed in ingredients and technique, forgetting that the barkeep is supposed to make his or her guests feel at ease. Since the bartender is often the first service staffer encountered by restaurant guests, it's the bartender's job to set the evening's tone. Depending on the restaurant, the bartender may aim for an understated or a broadly comic vibe. So long as the mood's consistent with the setting and pleasing to the patrons, it's the appropriate choice.

In many restaurants, the bartender's duties overlap with the manager's. By virtue of his or her perch – and because he or she interacts with so many guests – the bartender usually has a very good feel for what's happening in the restaurant at any given moment. The bartender almost always knows which customer is likely to try getting fresh with his server, and which server is having trouble keeping up with her tables. When someone needs to break up a lewd escapade in the bathroom or hustle a pickled drinker into a cab (occasions which are in no way confined to lower-end restaurants), that someone is the bartender.

Although pay schemes vary by restaurant, bartenders typically earn a higher hourly wage than servers. And in addition to the tips they collect at the bar, they're "tipped out" by the servers, which means they collect a percentage of their sales at night's end in exchange for making drinks.

SOMMELIER

In certain cities, you can eat quite well and never meet a sommelier. Wine service is handled differently in different locales, but the traditional restaurant model calls for a dedicated wine steward. Whether or not the sommelier wears a tastevin, the sippy-cup-on-a-chain that's largely fallen out of favor, he or she is responsible for maximizing guests' wine experiences. That means he or she should be able to suss out customers' likes and dislikes and recommend a wine which pairs with both the food and the people eating it. The sommelier is also tasked with assembling a thoughtful, engaging

wine list which complements the restaurant's cuisine. Ideal-
ly, the list should also include a range of price points.

To earn the industry's top credentials, sommeliers have to
pass a legendarily difficult test. But for most diners, a sommelier's certification doesn't matter much. What's most important is that the sommelier – or the manager, bartender, or
senior server playing the part – is able to convey his or her
excitement about wine and introduce customers to regions
and varietals they might not otherwise consider.

There's a popular misconception that only guests who left
their Bentley with the valet should ask to speak to the sommelier. In fact, the sommelier's services are available to any
customer who's thirsty for something grape-based: Nobody
in the restaurant knows better which $40 bottle is best suit-
ed for your forthcoming cassoulet. If you're not approached
first, tell your server you'd like to consult with the sommelier.

And don't worry about impressing the sommelier with
your wine knowledge: He or she is paid to know more about
wine than you do. Often, it's not even especially useful to drop
varietal names, since a French syrah and an Australian syrah
are about as alike as you and your third cousin who lives in
Tuscaloosa. Instead, brief the sommelier on how much you
want to spend (sommeliers who give you any guff about a
two-digit budget are crummy sommeliers) and the qualities
you like best in a wine. If you subscribe to *Wine Spectator*,
you might use terms like "full-bodied" and "high acid," but
it's just as acceptable to ask for something zippy and bright. A
good sommelier will know what you mean.

HOSTESS

Almost without exception, the hostess is the least experienced member of the restaurant's staff. Still, that doesn't
mean her job is easy. (I'm dispensing with the "his or her"

convention here, because a male host is as rare as a 25-cent oyster. The cliché about managers hiring cute for the host stand holds startlingly true.)

In addition to checking phone messages and confirming reservations, the hostess has the opportunity to make enemies of guests and servers alike by deciding who gets which table when. Servers are tremendously invested in the seating schedule, because their take depends partly on how many times they can "turn" the tables in their assigned sections. If a table sits vacant for a long stretch – or, worse, if a family settles in for appetizers and sodas at 5 p.m. and is still snacking on mozzarella-stick debris at 8 p.m. (a practice known as "camping") – the server's hopes of turning the table twice before the kitchen closes at 9 p.m. are pretty much dashed.

Too many customers can also pose problems for a server: When a server is double-sat, meaning two different tables are seated in the same section simultaneously, the server may struggle to take and fulfill orders promptly, leading to poor tips from both parties.

Not every restaurant is divided into sections: A few restaurants use a group-service model, in which everybody waits on everybody. If you're a basketball fan, it's like zone defense compared to man-to-man. Or so the theory goes: In reality, it can be difficult to secure a side of ranch dressing when nobody is specifically responsible for your welfare. And you'll invariably be offered dessert by at least three different servers. Smaller restaurants may opt for a rotation system in which Thelma waits on the first table, Bernice waits on the second, and Ernestine waits on the third, no matter where the guests sit.

But if the restaurant's sectioned off, the hostess strives to divvy up parties among fiefdoms: If you've ever been led to an obviously undesirable table at the start of the service, when almost every table is empty, the hostess' yearning for parity probably explains it.

The hostess monitors seating using a floor plan with numbered tables. There's no standardized numbering method for restaurants: Table 53 could be near the front door or near the kitchen. What's critical is that staffers know the numbers, so when a platter of burrata for table 53, seat 3 appears in the service window, anyone can take it to the guy in the blue polo shirt.

In order to estimate when the next table will become available, the hostess records when each table is sat. Many restaurants today don't take reservations, mostly because their margins are too small to risk wasting a table if the booking party doesn't show, so it's up to the hostess to soothe impatient guests and wheedle them into less-than-preferable seating schemes. Whether or not she's amenable to bribes is highly dependent on the restaurant's and surrounding community's mores. Keep an eye on your fellow customers for guidance: While it's probably wise to refrain from buying your way to a better experience if you plan to review the restaurant, you should note in your write-up if the hostess' palms are drippy with grease (and remember to hit the ATM before your next meal there).

RUNNER

The runner is the expediter's right-hand man, charged with delivering dishes to tables. But since there isn't always food ready to journey from the kitchen to the dining room, the runner is frequently enlisted for odd jobs such as filling water glasses, sweeping up puddles of Cheerios, and fetching more mustard from the storeroom.

BUSSER

The runner's all-important opposite, the busser, clears dishes from tables. If the runner is affiliated with the expo, the busser belongs to the dishwasher. Because the busser is already dealing with gristle, spittle, and balled-up napkins, he or she tends to draw the messier chores which crop up during service. Bussers empty kitchen trash cans which threaten to overflow in the middle of dinner rush; fix clogged toilets; and pick up the pieces when a wine bottle breaks.

SERVER

If "restaurant jobs" was a *Family Feud* category, "server" would show up at the top of the board. Serving is the quintessential restaurant occupation, held by more than a quarter of a million men and women in California alone.

As anyone who's eaten out knows, the server takes food and drink orders and brings a check at meal's end. But a server who did no more than that would soon be out of a job. In addition to the work they do before and after service, servers are also expected to anticipate and meet a customer's every need at table. A good server will proffer a black linen napkin to a customer wearing black pants; ask if you need hot sauce for your beans; and, without being asked, bring extra bread for the broth left in the bottom of a steamed-mussel bowl.

The best servers are calm, polite, and somehow always nearby when you want something. Yet a server's most important attribute is his or her expertise. Just as a server acts as your emissary to the kitchen, emphasizing the severity of your peanut allergy and explaining how hot you'd like your soup, a server is also the chef's proxy on the floor. With so many contemporary menus written in befuddling fashion – what is "spot prawn, daikon, horchata gelée"? Is it liquid? Solid? Spicy? Sweet? – it's up to the server to guide you toward the dishes you'll like best and steer you away from those which just don't work. At any decent restaurant, the servers have tasted every dish on the menu, and should be able to speak knowledgeably about them.

And if you're stuck with a reticent server, there's nothing wrong with asking questions. Open-ended questions are especially useful: What dish can't I miss? Which dish do you wish more people would order? Servers were foodies before the word was invented, and will usually seize any opportunity to swap culinary shoptalk with an interested customer. The surest way to score great service is to telegraph that you're after a good time and trust your server to lead you to it.

Talking about food is easily the best part of a server's job. The side-work that occurs at the start and end of a shift is considerably less fun: At most restaurants, servers arrive at least an hour before the restaurant opens to fill sugar caddies, clean bathroom mirrors, polish glasses, mop the floor, and do whatever else it takes to make the restaurant presentable. And when the restaurant's last guests leave, the routine repeats in reverse; servers roll silverware in paper napkins, marry ketchups, gather up salt shakers, and sweep the floor.

Whether or not they're waiting on customers, servers earn the same hourly wage, which – in most states – is far below the mandated minimum wage. According to federal law, tipped employees can be paid as little as $2.13 an hour. Servers make the bulk of their income through tips.

Which raises the eternal question: How much should you tip? There's lots of online chatter about whether a tip should be calculated before or after tax, and whether alcohol should count toward the tip total. Honestly, skinflints who concern themselves with such technicalities probably shouldn't be dining out. Yes, it's cheaper to eat at home. But restaurants offer all kinds of perks which can't be bought in a grocery store, and a tip is the toll you pay to enjoy them. Tip 20 percent on the entire bill. If the server was extraordinary or you feel like you can spare it, tip more. If your dinner cost $100, the difference between an unacceptable 15 percent tip and an industry-standard 20 percent tip is the same as the price of the coffee you reflexively ordered with dessert.

"Hey, now," penny-pinchers are bound to say. "Wasn't 15 percent considered a good tip just a few years ago? Sure. But times change. In 2003, people drank appletinis and ate gluten. Today the reigning tip amount is 20 percent.

Admittedly, there are servers who deserve to have their tips docked. But a tip is not a referendum on the restaurant: If you didn't like your food, or the room was too loud, or a cook bumped into you on your way back from the bathroom, the server's not to blame. Skimpy tips should be reserved for server errors, such as rudeness or flightiness which resulted in your being served chicken salad when you asked for fried chicken.

Understanding the roles restaurant workers play will enhance the credibility of your reviews and allow you to more effectively dissect your restaurant experiences. Yet even if you know what every restaurant staffer is supposed to do, it's still sometimes hard to figure out whose fault it is when a problem arises. Fortunately, the job descriptions outlined above make more sense when put in motion. Let's visit The Standard in the company of a pair of guests and see what happens.

•

Restaurant marketers devote long hours to figuring out why people patronize restaurants. Are they seeking value or luxury? Conviviality or elegance? Adventure or comfort? A quick tally of the chain-restaurant ads broadcast during an average prime-time television hour reveals the many different an-swers reached through extensive, expensive research.

As for Debbie and Denise, they're headed to The Standard because they're hungry. The former colleagues and current tennis partners had planned to meet for a late-afternoon drink, but now they're craving something more substan-tial than cocktail peanuts. Neither woman has ever dined at The Standard, but they've heard the ambience is conducive to quiet conversation, and Debbie's favorite farmers-mar-ket vendor swears by a gazpacho the chef makes with his early-season peaches.

When Debbie and Denise enter The Standard, the host stand is unattended. The restaurant usually schedules two hostesses on busy nights, but the manager had forecast very little traffic, assuming nasty weather would keep most folks at home. Now the lone hostess is seating a party of six, which can't quite get settled because none of the guests wants to sit in the booth's back-most corner, and one of the men can't decide where to stash his cane. That leaves nobody to greet Debbie and Denise.

Two or three minutes pass before the hostess scurries back to her post. She apologizes profusely for her absence and for not having a table available: Although Debbie and Denise see lots of empty tables, they apparently belong to diners with reservations. The hostess offers to add them to the wait list: She annotates the unfamiliar last name with a description which will help her find them in the bar, taking care to keep her adjectives benign, since guests take offense when they peer over her shoulder to find the phrase "fat man, cheap coat" written alongside their names. The hostess surveys the two-tops – with so many customers angling for tables, she can't waste a four-top on a party of two – to determine which groups will soon ask for a check. She notices dessert on two tables, and estimates Debbie and Denise will have to wait about 25 minutes.

The bar's as busy as the dining room. But the bartender says hello to Debbie and Denise as soon as they sit down, giving them water and a single cocktail menu; there are as many menus as bar stools, but most of the menus are now with guests seated in the dining room. When the bartender finally returns, having gotten waylaid by a server who needed change for a $100 bill, Denise asks for a mojito. The heretofore friendly bartender briefly scowls: Muddling mint is slow going, and he needs extra time to change a keg. He recovers quickly, though, producing Denise's mojito, Debbie's glass of vinho verde, and a genuine-seeming smile.

Debbie's not crazy about her wine. It has an off-putting funk that suggests the bottle's been open too long. The bartender notices she's pushed her glass away, and asks whether anything's wrong. Before she can finish explaining, he's whisked away the glass and replaced it with a wine list. With his back to customers, he samples the wine with a straw – confirming Debbie's suspicions – and tosses the bottle. Waste drives up costs, but he can't serve flawed wine. This time Debbie asks the bartender for a recommendation: He pours her tasting portions of a dry Riesling and a Sauvignon Blanc.

The hostess is fervently hoping the bartender is keeping the women happy, since it's been 40 minutes since she issued her 25-minute promise. The diners who appeared to be finishing up haven't gone anywhere, despite the busser's attempt to coax them toward the door by clearing everything off their tables but the salt and pepper shakers.

Finally, a table's ready. The server is keeping out of the weeds by running on autopilot: She asks Debbie and Denise whether they've dined at The Standard before; recites a list of specials; and warns that the kitchen's run out of asparagus.

But she leaves without remarking on Debbie and Denise's nearly emptied drinks.

Although the server urged them to order small plates for sharing, Debbie and Denise each prefer to have their own entrée, so Debbie gets the steak salad and Denise gets the roasted chicken. They opt to split the first course, though, agreeing on the Mediterranean grilled prawns. They also order another round of drinks.

Denise hates the shrimp dish. The tomato sauce is perked up with so much crushed red pepper that she's tempted to drain her second cocktail. Denise isn't completely adverse to spice, but when she orders Thai food, she rarely strays beyond two-star heat. This sauce is a healthy distance from Denise's comfort zone. Since Denise isn't as forward as Debbie, she doesn't say anything to the server, but silently wonders why the server didn't warn them the dish was seriously spicy.

As it turns out, the server didn't know. The Standard was one line cook short this evening, so the prep cook agreed to work a double. Unfamiliar with the appetizer, he avalanched it with way too much red pepper. If Denise had visited the restaurant yesterday or returns tomorrow, she'd be served a very different dish.

Eager to move on to their entrées, the women train their eyes on the runner's tray. But their dishes never seem to appear upon it. They wonder if the server forgot to place their order, or if she's just slow to pick it up. But if they were to wander back to the kitchen, they'd find their server pleading with the grill guy for the steak for Debbie's salad. His copy of the ticket fell to the floor while he was flipping a dozen burgers for a softball team enjoying post-game beers; now the roast chicken's been sitting under the heat lamp for more than five minutes, and he hasn't yet pulled the salad-bound beef from the cooler.

When the salad's ready, the expediter tells the line to re-
place the wilted greens alongside the chicken, and then
sends the completed order out with the manager, who sin-
cerely apologizes for the delay. "Hot plate," she warns Denise
as she places the chicken before her. But it's the salad which
poses a problem: Debbie had specifically asked for the dressing on the side.

The server had correctly notated Debbie's request, but the
salad station didn't heed it, and neither the expediter nor the
manager checked the tardy salad against the ticket before
serving it. While the salad is being remade, Denise starts in
on her chicken, which she deems excellent. The manager
brings Debbie an order of edamame to tide her over.

At the end of the meal (Debbie was gaga for her undressed
salad), there aren't too many dessert options from which to
choose. The pastry chef had predicted a slow night, too, so
the tortes and crème brûlées she prepared were sold out by
8 p.m. Debbie and Denise aren't interested in carrot cake,
so they ask their server to split the check – a reasonable request when there are only two people at the table – and pay
up. Debbie doesn't give much more thought to the meal, but
Denise is mentally replaying every moment which struck her
as significant. She's planning to write an online review of The
Standard.

Later we'll learn what Denise wrote. But before delving
into the nuts and bolts of online restaurant reviewing, it's
worth exploring the grand tradition of food criticism, which
existed long before the Internet. Because while sites such as
Yelp, Urbanspoon, and TripAdvisor may be brand-new, the
legacy which their users inherit is older than the cast-iron
stove.

CHAPTER 2

A Short History of Restaurant Criticism

HUMANS WERE LIKELY CRITICIZING FOOD long before they'd figured out how to prepare it. A 2006 study conducted at the Edinburgh Zoo revealed that captive chimpanzees make different noises when presented with various snacks: Louis and his fellow chimps reliably grunted more enthusiastically for chow than carrots.

As hominids acquired fire and language, their culinary assessments grew increasingly more sophisticated. The ancient Greek grammarian Athenaeus, among the Western world's first serious food writers, peppered his detailed accounts of banquets with opinions on the best-tasting fish in the Nile (*narka*, an electric catfish) and the proper method for preserving oysters. But it took another millennium or so for restaurant criticism to emerge, since society first had to invent the restaurant.

The restaurant, as reviewers know it, was originally a

French phenomenon, rooted in the Enlightenment fervor for self-betterment and healthy living. According to Rebecca Spang, author of *The Invention of the Restaurant*, Mathurin Roze de Chantoiseau in 1766 had the bright idea to serve restorative meat broths to wealthy Parisians. When the rage for bouillon fizzled, proprietors of *restoratif* houses – many of them former kitchen servants whose aristocratic employers had been deposed by the French revolution – shifted their focus to rich dishes and emphasized the quirky conventions that had grown up around the city's distinctive soup service. Since public eating previously had been confined to taverns and boarding houses, where meals were treated as utilitarian necessities, it became de rigueur for tourists from beyond Paris to come gawk at the restaurants' individual tables and printed menu cards.

Alexandre Balthazar Laurent Grimod de La Reynière, though, wasn't as easily impressed. A well-known bon vivant, the tubby Grimod was born in 1758 to noble parents who were so disgusted by his congenitally deformed hands – his right hand looked like a webbed pincer, his left resembled a lobster's claw – that they circulated the story that he'd been dropped in a pen with vicious pigs. Yet once outfitted with prosthetics designed by a Swiss clockmaker, Grimod could grasp a pen and fork, the tools he used to fashion himself as France's leading arbiter of culinary correctness.

Before the revolution, Grimod mostly busied himself with hosting lavish parties, including a feast at which the guest of honor was a pig dressed in the elder Grimod's clothes. After the Revolution, Grimod needed a job. He'd already failed at shopkeeping and the law, so he wrote theater reviews, stoking his interest in fine dining with frequent visits to the city's restaurants. Worried that the newly rich couldn't fully appreciate the establishments or discern the differences among them, he suggested to his publisher that what Parisian eaters really needed was a reliable guide to help them make wise restaurant choices. The first *Almanach de Gourmands* appeared in 1803; the book sold 20,000 copies.

For future editions of the *Almanach*, Grimod put together a panel of diners who convened once a week: Local restaurateurs were invited to deliver free food to the jury, with the promise of good reviews for deserving submissions. The men ate well for 465 straight Tuesdays.

Grimod published his final *Almanach* in 1813, complaining that he was exhausted by a decade of serving as Paris' palate. Historians suspect he may have been driven out of reviewing by competition, since a new crop of restaurant critics had begun to chime in with their opinions about the city's best values and most underrated chefs. Contemporaries such as Jean Anthelme Brillat-Savarin (of "Tell me what you eat, and I will tell you what you are" fame) were already tweaking Grimod's model to address ambience as well as cuisine, making sure diners wouldn't waste their time or money on lousy meals.

Still, restaurant criticism remained primarily an upper-class, urban preoccupation for nearly a century. Then in 1900, two brothers in the tire business released their first Michelin Guide, directing France's 3,000 drivers to the garages, toilets, hotels, and restaurants they'd need when venturing far from home. By 1920 – the same year that André and Édouard Michelin first slapped a price on the popular blue book – the guide's restaurant section was so popular that the publishers recruited a team of anonymous inspectors to grade restaurants, standardizing a practice that Grimod had tried before rejecting it in favor of his kitchen cabal. In 1926, Michelin started issuing a single star to particularly worthy restaurants; the current three-star rating system was inaugurated in 1936.

In the U.S., travelers relied on Duncan Hines for restaurant recommendations. Hines, a traveling salesman, started work in an era when fatal food poisoning was considered a legitimate job hazard. He started taking careful notes on restaurants which met his sanitation standards, eventually filling a notebook with hundreds of names. Fellow salesmen headed to Topeka or Buffalo got in the habit of calling Hines before hitting the road; after a Chicago paper wrote a feature about Hines' curious hobby, regular folks started doing the same. Hines in 1935 was so overwhelmed by the phone calls, letters, and telegrams that he compiled a list of 167 "superior places" in 30 states and slipped copies into the family Christmas card, assuming that would quell the clamor. Hardly.

"We got hundreds of requests for cards from people we had never heard of," Hines said in an interview recounting the genesis of *Adventures in Good Eating*, quoted in Louis Hatchett's *Duncan Hines: The Man Behind The Cake Mix*. "It made me realize that we had done something that had never been tried in this country – because there were no authoritative and unbiased guides to good eating. I felt that I could perform a real service to the public by giving them an appreciation of fine food and telling them where they could get a decent meal."

Americans loved Hines for his integrity: He dined anonymously, using a 20-year-old portrait to illustrate his book, and never accepted a free meal. As Hatchett wrote, "If Duncan Hines said a particular restaurant meal made a man wish for hollow legs, it did. And there was no argument about it."

Hines understood the sensual value of nostalgic dishes such as beaten cream biscuits and fried yellow-legged chickens, but his write-ups were largely free of contention because he was always most interested in cleanliness and surroundings which would strike the weary salesman as cheery. Gri-

mod probably wouldn't have considered him a suitable partner for a conversation about mother sauces.

Craig Claiborne, on the other hand, was fascinated by the
food. In 1962, Claiborne, *The New York Times'* food editor, de-
buted a weekly column featuring "New York restaurants that
are recommended on the basis of varying merits." A year later, he added star ratings to the mix. Claiborne had previously
reviewed the odd important restaurant, but his commitment
to independently assessing a wide range of restaurants on a
weekly basis jump-started the modern age of food criticism.
By the end of the decade, nearly every major U.S. paper had
hired a restaurant reviewer.

Claiborne wasn't swayed by fanciness: He steered his
readers to mom-and-pop pizzerias, Greek diners, and – in his
very first column – a Chinese restaurant in Harlem. While he
was forgiving of pomp (his 1975 chronicle of a $4,000 Pari-
sian meal outraged *Times'* readers who considered the escapade in poor taste at the height of a recession), his egalitarian
streak informed much of the most important restaurant writing of the late 20th century. Claiborne's philosophical influ-
ence is evident in the work of Jane and Michael Stern, who
in 1977 published their Americana-rich *Roadfood*, and in the
writing of Jonathan Gold, who in 1986 started nosing around
Los Angeles' ethnic neighborhoods for *LA Weekly*.

Although Claiborne put newspapers in the restaurant-reviewing business, daily journalism (and glossy magazines
such as the late *Gourmet*) didn't have a monopoly on smart
criticism. Some of the most astute commentary flourished
on the food world's fringes: In 1971, Seymour Britchky intro-
duced his New York City newsletter *The Restaurant Reporter*,
jamming it with imagery that captivated the pickiest eaters
and sharp phrases that comforted cynics. Years later, future
Village Voice critic Robert Sietsema recorded his NYC eating

expeditions in a homemade zine that sold for $10 a year.

Independent eaters next shifted their chronicling efforts to the Internet. In 1997, Jim Leff and Bob Okumura created Chowhound, an online discussion board for amateur food scouts looking to trade tips. Trusting non-credentialed, unnamed diners for restaurant advice wasn't an entirely novel phenomenon: In 1979, Tim and Nina Zagat surveyed 200 friends for restaurant opinions after deciding their hometown paper's critic was unreliable, distilling their responses into blurbs pierced with terse quotes. Zagat now publishes "popular" guides to "hot" restaurants in 100 "culinary capitals," aggregating reviews from nearly half a million consumers. But Zagat contributions are mediated by an editorial team; on Chowhound, diners were free to pronounce their own views with very little interference by site moderators.

Chowhound and eGullet, an interactive site launched in 2001, were the primary outlets for amateur reviews throughout the early aughts. But in 2005, MRL Ventures restarted a site which was intended to challenge the Yellow Pages (remember those?). Within three years, Yelp was attracting 10 million visitors a month. Growth has only picked up since, with the number of posted reviews surging by 45 percent in 2012. What's not yet clear is whether those reviews – and the regular folks responsible for them – will shape culinary culture as dramatically as the writings of Grimod, Hines, Claiborne, and Gold.

CHAPTER 3

Where Online Reviews Go Awry

PEOPLE WHO DON'T WRITE ABOUT restaurants, either for pay or passion, tend to believe that professional critics and online reviewers are mortal enemies. I've fielded countless calls from reporters trying to goad me into bad-mouthing Yelpers. I've disappointed them all.

While I fret that readers don't always understand the difference between a restaurant review based on two or more anonymous, unannounced visits and a review based on ordering a turkey sandwich at Aunt Sally's birthday lunch, I don't blame online review writers for the confusion. (That said, food bloggers who threaten to post bad reviews if they don't receive special treatment deserve all the spit that chefs put in their dishes.) To the contrary, I'm enormously grateful for the legwork that amateurs do.

Yelp is quick to bestow elite status on reviewers who habitually post the first assessment of a new restaurant, which makes the site the single best source of information about just-opened venues beyond the mainstream. It's impossible for a food critic to routinely stalk the streets of a major city, sussing out every recent addition to the restaurant landscape. Nor can critics stuck at their newsroom desks rely on every restaurant having the financial wherewithal to place ads or circulate press releases announcing their arrival. And even restaurants with actual advertising budgets may limit their buys to the foreign-language press, a good business decision which inevitably galls food writers trying to track down the region's top Korean dumplings. For all these reasons, online reviews that flag brand new restaurants are indispensable.

As a food critic, I'm not especially interested in what online reviewers think of a particular restaurant. I occasionally discover hobbyists who know their stuff, and I might click through all of their reviews to learn what's impressed them lately. But I'm more likely to use Yelp as a facts cache, trolling reviews of unfamiliar restaurants for mentions of dishes, dining rooms, or service strategies which merit further investigation: Just because an online reviewer is turned off by goat lasagna doesn't mean I don't want to try it.

Sometimes I'll browse online reviews haphazardly, calling up random restaurant names and cuisines which sound intriguing. More often, though, I'll skew a search in my favor by crunching census data to figure out exactly which local neighborhood is home to a sizable number of immigrants from a certain country. Then I run a Yelp search within that ZIP code for restaurants specializing in food from their homeland. It's not a fail-safe method, but it at least feels like a remarkably modern way to explore an eating scene.

I'm forever designing searches for Mexican restaurants, not because they're hard to find – even in Seattle, a city in which only six out of every 100 residents identifies as Latino,

the phone book lists more than 300 Mexican restaurants –
but because there are so dadgum many of them. And to com-
pound the problem, one strip-mall Mexican joint looks pretty
much like another. Perhaps my colleagues further south are
more practiced sleuths, but I have no way of intuiting when
genius lurks behind maracas-shaped cardboard cutouts and
neon *cerveza* signs. A restaurant might serve a sauce that's essentially unknown outside of Puebla or quesadillas smeared
with *xoconostle,* but it takes a healthy dose of dumb luck (or
the kind of time that's not available to food writers living in
the 24-hour news cycle) to find it. Enter Yelp.

Off-the-radar restaurants give online reviewers an opportunity to shine, since they own the discussion of them. An
ambitious Yelper could invest tremendous seriousness and
thought in a write-up of a restaurant helmed by a *Food &
Wine* Best New Chef, but I'll always turn first to a professional critic's assessment. Whether or not I agree with his or her
opinions, I'm at least acquainted with the reviewer's credentials, methodology, and preferences. I know that if a specific
critic hates a restaurant, I'm bound to love it, which is a certainty I can't wring from Yelp. Yet too many online reviewers
bungle their big chance, committing elementary errors that
render their all-important reviews of unsung restaurants use-
less at best – and misleading at worst.

Recently, I stumbled upon a Yelp listing for a Mexican
restaurant which strummed every string of my *guitarrón.* Lo-
cated on an auxiliary street that's a better bet for rental vid-
eos and home health-care equipment than quality food, the
family-owned restaurant had won online accolades for its sophisticated moles and standing special of slow-roasted lamb
shanks. Online reviewers agreed that the restaurant stood
near the pinnacle of Mexican cookery in the area, collectively
awarding it 4.5 out of 5 stars (for more on the business of as-

signing stars, stay tuned for Chapter 7).

Our meal was awful. Not just "I wonder what folks like about this restaurant?" awful, but "Should we worry for the fate of humanity?" awful. There was absolutely nothing praiseworthy about the restaurant. Still, the experience was instructive: When I later reread the Yelp posts, it was clear that the writers had committed a spate of cardinal sins common to online reviewing. I made the mistake of falling for them, but there's no reason you should make the mistake of repeating them. Here, the eight errors you should strive to avoid on Yelp, with examples drawn verbatim from the Yelp reviews which seduced me:

1. The underreported review

"Got inside, and the staff was so friendly and I had pork casa...or something like that and it was wonderful. Everyone in my party had a wonderful meal, except the chicken was a little dry. This is not a fancy Mexican restaurant, but the price, food quality, service and quantity of the meal, I give this place 5 stars."

If I told you I was just back from the most amazing vacation, you might be tempted to book a trip to the same destination. But you'd probably be significantly less inclined to follow my lead if I told you I couldn't recall whether I'd been in Hawaii or Haiti.

Accuracy matters. Before you can tackle the thorny issues posed by passing judgment on someone else's handiwork, you first need to get your facts straight. "Pork casa... or something like that" may fall on the extreme end of the uninformed spectrum, but it's shocking how many online reviewers don't bother to carefully record the most important elements of their eating-out experience. We'll return to the topic of fact-gathering in Chapter 5.

2. The clichéd review

"Their carne asada is one of the best I have had. They also make an excellent tamale that is moist and succulent just as a tamale should be. Their rice I swear has crack in it because it's delicious and addictive, not bland and oversalted like most mexican rices. MMmmmm mmmm."

This reviewer wins points for explaining exactly why she's so fond of the restaurant's Mexican rice, but the power of her write-up is diluted by an overreliance on clichéd descriptors and imagery. Clichés aren't necessarily harmful, but it's hard to capture an experience or engage a reader's attention with overused and inexact phrasing.

Descriptors which are rarely encountered outside of food writing, such as "succulent," "delectable," "luscious," "toothsome," and "scrumptious," should always be avoided. The same goes for cutesy words from the yum-o school of foodspeak, such as "delish" and "sammies," as well as words which suggest eating is a wicked act, such as "sinful" and "decadent."

If I had my druthers, "moist" would make the banned list, too. I've made a point of never using it in my reviews, mostly because I think the word's unappetizing and imprecise. But I get why "moist" made the canon. There's just no way around certain words when writing about food.

Even the most talented reviewers are bound to use adjectives such as "salty" more than once in the course of a full-length column, because there are no perfect synonyms for them. It's not quite right to call a burger briny, for instance, unless the patty's threaded with seaweed. And brackish doesn't work either. Fortunately, the paucity of words in the

food critic's pantry forces writers to fool around with meta-
phors and similes that make for good reading.

But images can be equally shopworn. I'd wager there
wasn't a single reader of the above review who'd never before
heard food compared to crack. Other expressions to avoid include "licked the plate clean," "made my mouth water," "party
in my mouth," and "MMmmmmmmmm." In Chapter 6, we'll
return to the topic of word choice and further discuss how to
write without clichés.

3. The flavorless review

*"I had carne asada tacos. They had tons of flavor. My hubby had a
tamale, taco and enchilada. I tasted the tamale and it was fabu-
lous. The kids loved it there too!!!"*

Most English speakers would agree that adjectives such as
amazing, wonderful, gorgeous, and exquisite have only positive connotations. Slang sometimes turns meanings around,
providing the fodder for sitcom plots which turn on Granny
not understanding why the kids call her casserole "totally
bad," but it's generally pretty clear whether a word's supposed to convey pleasure or displeasure.

Yet "flavorful," a favorite term of online reviewers, is de-
cidedly more ambiguous. Spoiled milk has a strong flavor.
So does a two-day old scallop. Granted, any adjective which
appears in close proximity to multiple exclamation points is
probably being used in complimentary fashion, but the word
itself reveals nothing. Did this reviewer's tacos have the flavor
of beef or burnt tires? It's unclear.

When writing about food, describing flavors is paramount.
It's also extraordinarily difficult, which is why we'll take up
flavor analysis in Chapter 8.

4. The worst review ever!

"I ordered the nachos with picadillo and they were easily some of the best nachos I've ever had. Lots of gooey cheese, picadillo, jalapenos, beans. So yum. My husband had the pollo a la crema, which he loved and said it was the best he'd had."

There's no way of knowing how many times this reviewer has eaten nachos in her lifetime. But considering the ubiquity of corn chips and processed cheese in the U.S. – Americans reportedly consume 6,000 tons of nachos on Super Bowl Sunday alone – it's reasonable to assume she's probably lost count of how many times she's sampled the snack. So to encounter "easily some of the best nachos I've ever had" is a very big deal.

Finding the best anything is an exceedingly rare experience. But the chances of stumbling upon your personal best nachos at the very same time that your husband's enjoying the best pollo a la crema of his life? Almost nil.

Exceptional and best aren't synonymous. That's true whether we're talking about food, sports, or just about anything else. For instance, as a native Michigander, I root for the Detroit Tigers. The Tigers' first baseman, Prince Fielder, is a phenomenal player. He's hit 269 home runs in his career, which is 269 more major league homers than most of us will ever hit. But he's not even the best player on his team. It doesn't undercut his achievements to refrain from randomly flinging around the word "best" when describing what he does.

There's nothing wrong with the qualified "best" or "worst." Maybe your nachos were dressed with the best picadillo you've discovered in your hometown, or perhaps your pollo a la crema was accompanied by one of the worst green salads you ever recall being served in a Mexican restaurant. But phrases such as "best I've ever had" should be reserved for special occasions, since the descriptor's meaningless when applied to every pleasing dish. We'll look at more trustworthy ways to convey enthusiasm in Chapter 7.

5. The one-sided review

"I don't know why this place gets such good reviews. The highly regarded salsa tasted like watery Tapatio. I had Arroz Con Pollo and it was the worst I've ever had. It was very saucy with too much rice and the meat and vegetables didn't seem like they were cooked very long. The flavor was also bland and the tortillas were warmed up grocery store quality."

Having eaten at the restaurant in question, I can confirm that this review is spot-on. But I didn't pay it much heed when I first read it, and imagine many other readers were similarly dismissive. That's because the writer's opinions deviated so dramatically from the consensus that I figured his or her conclusions were colored by hostility: Online reviewing sites inevitably attract kvetchers for whom nothing's ever good enough.

To avoid being misclassified as a member of that unpopular group, it's essential to explicitly acknowledge a restaurant's best qualities, even if the overall experience is irredeemably rotten. In the case of this Mexican restaurant, many of the upbeat reviews cited the dining room's family-friendly atmosphere. I wouldn't quibble with that point. Assuming this reviewer felt the same, he or she could have tempered criticism of the food with a factual line or two about the availability of booster seats or the host's easy way with children. Such commentary allows online reviewers to establish that they ate in the same restaurant as its fans and are capable of appreciating its merits – without ever treading into positive territory.

Reviewers writing raves of poorly rated restaurants should also strive to recognize their failings, lest readers think they have ulterior motives (read: an ownership interest) for flouting the norm. Partisanship is surely a lesser gaffe than clichéd writing or inaccurate reporting, but reviewers interested in preserving their credibility should make room in their write-ups for diplomacy. In Chapter 5, we'll explore how to puzzle out what's commendable about the most dismal restaurants.

6. The impressionistic review

"My wife complained about the taco tasting of old oil, otherwise it was good. Despite it exceeding my expectations, I thought the place was a bit cheesy and it was definitely overpriced. The portions are good size, though."

In my last reviewing gig, my primary competitor had a very different appetite than I did. Whenever I accused a restaurant of serving too-small portions, she'd fault the restaurant for putting more food on its plates than diners could possibly finish.

Restaurant-goers are bound to disagree over portions and fair prices: So long as eaters have differently sized stomachs and bank accounts, they'll never reach accord on the rightness of a $12 burrito. Fortunately, the online reviewer doesn't have to anticipate every possible opinion. By dealing in specifics, the review writer can forgo having to decide whether a dish is too costly or too measly.

A great review isn't merely a list of statistics. Many people eat out for fairly abstract reasons – perhaps they're drawn to glamour or love to people-watch – so it's silly to ignore restaurants' unquantifiable elements. But it's enormously helpful to provide objective information when available, such as the price of the calamari and the type of noodle used in the carbonara.

Rather than declare a restaurant "definitely overpriced," quote real numbers: Many restaurants specializing in global cuisines don't have comprehensive websites, so diners are reliant on online reviewers to tell them exactly how much they'll pay for dinner. More frequently, though, prices are already published elsewhere, which means it's better to focus energies on describing exactly what the money buys than on decreeing how much you'd charge for the dish.

Pricing is a nuanced art: Expensive food can be a good deal and cheap food can be a rip-off, since cost and value are two different considerations. But portioning often plays into diners' value calculations, so instead of describing a portion as a "good size," supply a useful comparison. Was the burrito smaller than a bookmark? Bigger than an oven mitt?

Readers may be interested in your opinion, but they're especially interested in how you reached it: Chapter 4 will cover in further detail the tricky business of backing up what you say.

7. The emotional review

"Our favorite Mexican Resturant. The staff always remember us and treat us well. If we attend without a family member the owner's not only notice but will ask us to say hello to that missing member. Our family visit's on a somewhat regular basis now."

Putting aside the spelling and grammatical errors that mar the above review, it's a fine example of an online reviewer evaluating his or her personal experience instead of the restaurant as a whole. There are endless examples of angry reviewers basing their reviews on momentary outrages, but happy reviewers are equally apt to be swayed by emotions. A hostess who's generous with her hugs? Love it!

It's very hard to criticize a restaurant run by good people: According to other online reviews, the owners of the restaurant in question have also sent home guests with mints and flowers, stopped toddlers from eating spicy food, and waited outside in the rain with a container of sour cream after accidentally omitting it from a take-out fajita order. But online reviews are read primarily by locals and tourists looking for a meal, not an ongoing relationship. Since it's possible to have a great experience at a bad restaurant – and vice versa – thinking about the bigger picture is crucial when summing up a restaurant for potential customers. We'll take a closer look at how that process works in Chapter 10.

8. The egotistical review

"My husband and I are from Central California and have pretty high expectations of Mexican food. We haven't found anything amazing or that really compares to what we are used to but this restaurant was clean, the food was good and the staff are VERY friendly!"

As I already mentioned, I was born in Michigan, which led the nation in cherry production when I was a kid. Still, I don't consider myself an expert on cherry pie. Culinary knowledge is not a birthright. Sure, Californians and Texans have undoubtedly eaten more Mexican food than most of their neighbors in the Pacific Northwest. But bad Mexican food is bountiful in those states, too: Eating scads of greasy queso is a weak substitute for real *cocina* savvy. Unfortunate-

ly, too many online reviewers have developed the bad habit
of suggesting their opinions are sacrosanct because of their
heritage.

Like many white Midwesterners, I learned to drive before
I learned how to eat sushi. My hometown's first Japanese
restaurant didn't open until the 1980s – and it took about a
decade for my friends and me to screw up the courage to eat
there.

Since that initial sashimi date, I've eaten in countless
stateside sushi bars, izakayas, and noodle shops. But at this
rate, it's unlikely I'll ever catch up to an eater who lived in Ja-
pan or was reared on its cuisine. Even if I ate ramen every day
for the rest of my life, I'd probably still understand the dish
differently than someone who couldn't recall his or her first
bowlful. Such is the nature of memory and taste.

But that doesn't mean I'm unequipped to assess tonkotsu
broth. On the contrary, my lack of nostalgia may be a boon
when it comes to objective assessment. As former *Voice* critic
Robert Sietsema told a gathering of Association of Food Journalists members: "I thought it would be interesting to ask a
Mandarin person to go to a Mandarin restaurant. Not only
were they honored, they loved the role. But a lot of people
who come from the country of the food you're eating, you'd
be surprised how narrow their perspective is."

Most important, it's not especially helpful to tell Seattle
readers that a restaurant isn't as good as a restaurant in a far-
off state, since very few eaters are torn between having dinner in their neighborhood or flying to El Paso for the evening.
While it's always a good idea to contextualize opinions, it's
not fair to assume diners are familiar with Mexican restaurants 900 miles south of home. We'll address more useful
comparisons in the next chapter.

CHAPTER 4

Deconstructing the Review

WITH SO MANY PITFALLS TO avoid, restaurant reviewing can seem like a very daunting task. The good news is that almost everybody feels similarly scared when they're starting out: After all, anxiety is the difference between typing and writing.

The bad news is, it never gets much better: I've written hundreds of reviews, and I still get nervous on review-writing days. I've tried to facilitate the writing process by adopting predictable routines – I eat take-out tofu pho, drink a liter of Crazy Water No. 3 mineral water, and listen to the same six songs on repeat – but there's no way around the angst that arises when you're constantly checking your work for evidence of the missteps outlined in the previous chapter. Even when I'm having fun with a review, I'm asking myself whether the last paragraph was too self-referential or overly huffy. I'll scour every sentence for a cliché I can eliminate, and rework a peach pie description until it's precise enough to please a clinical chemist.

Yet I somehow always manage to get my reviews written. I've reprinted one below so we can examine the various components of a complete review. Considering the fundamental differences between full-length print reviews and online reviews, it's fair to wonder whether the lessons of the former are applicable to the latter. My feeling is there's a great deal to be gleaned from professional reviews, including an appreciation of structure, descriptive details, imagery, and balance.

Perhaps it's a reflection of my industry bias, but I strongly suspect the quality of online reviews would perk up if more writers put print reviews on their regular reading lists. It doesn't much matter whether the review concerns a restaurant in your hometown or a city which you've never visited: Just as you probably deign to look at paintings which originated in far-off locales, you'll want to acquaint yourself with criticism from other places.

Although I tend to write more positive and middling reviews than negative reviews (a fortunate by-product of living in a great food city), I think it makes good sense to analyze a column chock full of reservations. Because online reviewers are highly motivated to chronicle their most disappointing experiences, and because pans handled in an irresponsible manner can do real and lasting damage, it's important to know how to do negative right. But since this review's subject may have improved since I made my three visits in early 2013, I've omitted identifying information. We'll call the restaurant XYZ.

The first restaurant you'll meet, though, isn't XYZ, but a significantly humbler eatery called Mehak. As you'll read, Mehak was drawn into the discussion for the sake of fairness, accuracy, and efficacy. Finally, a note on length: This review clocks in at 1,100 words, which is significantly longer than the standard online review. Heck, it's significantly longer than most daily-newspaper restaurant reviews. But the same principles would apply if the review was one-tenth the size (350 words is pretty close to ideal for an online restaurant review). The original review is in *italics;* annotations are in plain text.

Review of Restaurant XYZ

The lifeblood of Mehak Indian Cuisine is delivery, as the Northgate restaurant's interior makes abundantly clear. The sheer white curtains and tablecloths look as though they've been dipped in weak tea, the salmon-pink wall paint has faded to a canned-tuna hue, and the ratty Berber carpet isn't perfectly flush with the floor. The dining room's sparsely ornamented with a mirror and a coat stand, although a back room that a fancier restaurant might make its storage closet is crammed with cots, games, and a huge plastic tub of salty snacks. In addition to being a takeout hub, Mehak is a home.

And we're off, with descriptions galore. While taste is the prevailing sense in food reviews, trying to explain a restaurant without referencing its sights, smells, and sounds is flat-out foolish. It's worth taking a moment during a meal to focus exclusively on what you hear, smell, and feel. Is your chair lumpy? What song is playing on the radio? Can you smell frying oil? These are the sorts of details which can make a write-up pop. Fortunately, visual details are easier than ever to filch with the help of a camera phone: Consider shooting interiors which aren't suitable for posting, but which will jog your memory when you can't recall the exact shade of the wall.

Speaking of shades, note that the color images in the above paragraph allude to foods. Although the speaker of

Shakespeare's Sonnet 18 ultimately decides not to compare his love to a summer day, his initial instincts were good, since everyone – including folks who live in rainy, gray Seattle – is familiar with a sunny August morning. Imagery only works if it's broadly accessible.

Yet guests who make the trek to Mehak anyhow will be rewarded by a warmth that can't be exported in a Styrofoam box. When owner Mit Kaur brings a plate of chicken tikka masala to your table, she squeezes your shoulder with bear-hug intensity: "Welcome," she says. Soon, perhaps, the two of you could be playing cards and eating pretzels.

Kaur speaks English haltingly, but if you ask, she'll lead you through her kitchen to the tandoor, a fiery clay pit with crooked disks of naan affixed to its inner perimeter like lichens on a log. Peeled from the oven, the chewy bread is as impressive as the ancient contraption that produced it, its uneven surface ridged with air bubbles and bruised with smoke. This is naan too good to spend on sauce-sopping.

There are a zillion ways to start a review, but the most popular strategies can be grouped into a few general categories. For this quick survey of those styles, let's break away from my review of XYZ to look at leads written by other critics.

There's the **microscopic lead**, in which the writer opens by describing a representative dish in minute detail. For example, if a writer was particularly impressed by the kitchen's mischievous streak, she might begin by describing the pungency and heft of a sauerbraten smeared with gochujang. Here's *The New York Times*' Hungry City columnist, Ligaya Mishan, introducing readers to a pasta hall in the Chelsea Market:

The basket, made entirely of aged Parmigia-no-Reggiano, was pocked and porous like a growth of coral, flaring outward at the rim. Heaped within were snips of asparagus and translucent asparagus-ricotta ravioli, their milky green interiors showing through.

As described by the waiter, the dish had sounded suspect, a flashback to a cornier decade; none of the worldly New Yorkers at my table had wanted to order it. Now they leaned in, eyes bright.

A night at Giovanni Rana Pastificio & Cucina is this kind of dance: distrust of the restaurant's theme-park theatrics and grudging acknowledgment of your primal response to them.

—Ligaya Mishan, "Pasta That Comes With a Back Story," *The New York Times,* May 9, 2013

Alternately, there's the **macroscopic lead**, preferred by writers who like to outline a current trend or philosophy before showing how the restaurant under review illustrates it. Besha Rodell of *LA Weekly* took that very tack when sizing up Black Hogg:

Oh, dude food, what have you wrought?

A few years ago, at the beginning of the chef revolution, young cooks stopped cooking what was expected and started cooking what they wanted to eat. The resulting meat-centric, balls-out approach was both exciting and refreshing – bringing with it some of the last decade's most astonishing food. Suddenly spice, salt, fat, offal, cult seafood items, and stinky cheese became the norm. Restaurants that 10 years ago would have seemed like risky business prop-

ositions became the model for many young chef/
owners. You must have livers. You must have uni.
You must have octopus, belly meat, bacon in places
where no bacon has gone before.

This is certainly the tradition claimed by Eric Park,
the young chef behind Black Hogg in Silver Lake."

—Besha Rodell, "Black Hogg Down," *LA Weekly*,
Jan. 17, 2013

Want more? There's the **anecdotal lead**, which involves
the retelling of a revealing incident, such as a 10-minute
search for the restaurant's only corkscrew. When the *Village
Voice*'s Tejal Rao launched her review of Foragers City Table
by recounting a little girl's response to the menu, her readers
knew the restaurant had a daring edge:

A little girl is standing at the entrance to Foragers
City Table and reading the menu to her father as he
taps away on his BlackBerry. "Hey, Daddy, what's
crépinettes? What's yuzu? What's prickly ash?" He
doesn't know the answers, and he isn't in the mood
to look them up, so eventually they go elsewhere for
dinner.

It's a shame, because the new Chelsea restaurant
could have fed them well."

—Tejal Rao, "Something's in Store for You," *Village
Voice*, July 4, 2012

There's also the **humorous lead**, typically built around a
wry observation about the restaurant or contemporary dining
culture; the **memoir lead**, in which the writer dredges up a

bit of personal history to make a point; the **newsy lead**, which jumps right into the chef's resume or venue's background; and the **parody lead**, written in an imaginary character's voice. These four lead styles require the most preliminary research and literary sophistication; should you decide to use any of them, make sure your opener draws attention to the point you wish to make about the restaurant, not your restaurant-related accomplishments or frightfully clever phrasing.

Finally, there's the **scene-setting lead**, which was the lead of choice for my review of Restaurant XYZ, to which we'll return now. The key to pulling off the you-are-there opener is copious details: Not a box, but a Styrofoam box. Not a plate of food, but a plate of chicken tikka masala. Not snacks, but pretzels.

XYZ – which opened last December in South Lake Union, after what felt to Seattle's food-fixated tribe like an excruciatingly long wait – serves naan too. Unlike Mehak, XYZ is a restaurant to be seen: At the back end of its boxy dining room is a conspicuously posh lounge, furnished with exposed light bulbs, an elaborately cut-out cornice, scrolling wooden benches, and darker wooden tables of the same squat height. The naan, though, is considerably less baroque. XYZ's buttered triangles of prairie-flat bread taste like cut-rate pita that's been frozen and thawed, then frozen and thawed again. It's firm and flavorless, flaws not given much cover by the cold serving temperature. This is naan to make you sad.

Whoa, Mehak was a MacGuffin? Sort of. After three visits to XYZ, I knew the restaurant's story was summed up by its naan.

Every review should have an elevator pitch, or concise idea, propelling it. There's nothing wrong with working out

your thoughts in writing, but that draft isn't for public consumption: Before writing your review, you should settle on
a one-sentence version of the story you want to tell – even if
your final review runs only five or six sentences. Maybe the
restaurant you're reviewing is an oddly delicious example of
masculinity run amok. Maybe it's a testament to the grace of
self-taught cooks. Or maybe it's set to shake up the world of
country ham.

For me, XYZ fell sadly flat despite alpine expectations,
which made its miserable naan the perfect metaphor for the
restaurant. But I doubt I would have been as disappointed by
the naan if I hadn't tried better naan elsewhere; bringing Mehak into the mix made the comparison explicit and fair. While
that's more reporting than most online reviewers will want to
pursue, it's an example of how research and specificity can
strengthen a write-up. Even if you don't have the luxury of
taking a contrasting-naan field trip, you can help your readers by likening a dish to similar dishes served locally, assuming you're adequately familiar with them.

*As great chefs who've tried charging double-digit prices for
tacos have learned, there's a collective American reluctance to
pay serious money for dishes associated with the developing
world. Folks like their pho and falafel cheap. But a series of
accomplished restaurateurs – including XYZ's [owner], who
co-owns [a major city]'s critically acclaimed ABC with her husband – have helped diners understand there's nothing oxymo-
ronic about upscale Indian food. The cuisine's sophistication is
highly compatible with elegance and the price it commands.*

I'm very careful to not crowd my columns with too much
me, me, me, but it's worth stating your personal philosophy
– such as whether you've taken a blood oath never to pay $16

for a plate of red-lentil curry – if it has a bearing on your judgment.

So there's nothing theoretically wrong with a meal at XYZ costing four or five times as much as a meal at Mehak. What's regrettable is that in elevating dishes that eaters may recognize from takeout containers and steam-table buffets, XYZ has left behind a certain soulfulness. With its dreadful service, mangled dishes, and often irrational insistence on modernity, the ambitious restaurant has snuffed out the compelling energy that emanates from traditional tandoors.

If I had to cut this review down to 75 words for online posting, the preceding paragraph would do the trick.

The management team, always well represented on the floor when there wasn't a server available to take a drink order or a busser around to clear the previous course's plates, is apparently aware of the restaurant's troubles: During my two visits, they hovered around the open kitchen, looking as concerned as Ravens fans during the third quarter of the Super Bowl. [The owner] has also openly acknowledged problems, using her Twitter feed to apologize for equipment failures which hobbled XYZ's soft opening and, three weeks later, to advertise for cooks and a head chef. No restaurant's perfect out of the gate, of course. But it's rare for a restaurant with such an estimable pedigree to underwhelm so radically after months of service.

Super Bowl shtick works in a newspaper, which is timely by definition. Current events should probably be left out of online reviews.

The ABC name and desirable location have conspired to

keep XYZ very busy, and the restaurant's slatted wooden ceil-ing doesn't do much to muffle the crowd noise. On my first visit, the room's decibel level measured 86 on my smart-phone app, which is slightly louder than heavy city traffic. Fortunately, my server wasn't especially interested in carrying on an extended conversation. When I asked for recommendations, she zeroed in on an appetizer of sautéed onions and a short-rib entrée. "So I'll just put that in for you," she announced, pulling out her iTouch order pad without waiting for my response. I asked instead for a few more minutes to consider the menu, an act of disobedience that inadvertently made me memorable.

"Normally, I'd say that's too much food," the same server snarled when she took my return-visit order. "But I remember how much you packed away last time."

As much as I hate to muddle the message, sometimes you don't want to burden your review with too many details. Over the course of two visits, my server had lots to say. But it's pointless to recount every conversation or linger too long on a server who could very well quit her job (admittedly, that's putting a generous spin on it) before readers have a chance to eat at Restaurant XYZ.

Recognizing irrelevant details is as important as includ-ing the critical ones. All I needed to convey here was the style (iTouch order pad) and tone ("snarled") of service. I didn't need to expound upon what the server was wearing, what she was doing while I waited for my okra, or how I felt about being told I eat too much. Readers are a pretty sharp bunch.

None of the other staffers I encountered was quite so con-temptuous, but service issues abounded: One hapless runner was stuck with a plate of samosas that apparently didn't be-long to any of the tables he approached, while another reached around the used, stacked-up plates on our table to drop off more food. He left empty-handed.

Still, the restaurant's sloppy cooking is its ultimate undoing. Perhaps the best dish I sampled at XYZ was a griddled pura. Although its crowning tomatoes and onions were lost in a bacon haze, the crepe itself would be the pride of any Sunday-morning pancake flipper. But it was burdened with, as a server put it, "all the seasonings we use." The cumin, turmeric, coriander, and cardamom were applied in bizarre proportion, making the dish as off-kilter as a string quartet with three double basses and a violin.

Speaking of readers, I can't count on every reader being familiar with every cuisine I review. Honestly, *I'm* not always familiar with every cuisine I review, which is why my office is overflowing with cookbooks. All we eaters have to read up. But reviews aren't the proper forum for showing off what I've learned. Unfortunately, too many online review writers like to drone on about authenticity and esoteric food preparations. Personally, I'd rather compare an Indian crepe to a standard American pancake than waste words on its exact definition.

A pile of Brussels sprouts, sautéed to the leaf-shedding point, probably made sense on a spreadsheet: With cashews for crunch, paneer for silkiness, bell peppers for acid, and the sprouts for bitterness, the dish should have worked. But without any spice to stitch together its components, the dish tasted flat. Undercooked short ribs, slathered with a mahogany-colored tomato-cream curry, would have benefited from a shake of salt. Overcooked salmon needed more zip than a sheer curry of coconut and ginger offered.

Vegetarian dishes aren't safe bets either: Paneer, barely noticeable in the background of the Brussels sprouts preparation, doesn't have the star power to hold down a dish layered with tomatoes and onions. Instead, the dense, chalky cheese tastes like a co-op member's first stab at homemade tofu. And rubbery deviled eggs are stuffed with a curry so gritty it sticks in your teeth.

Better is the kale, jackfruit, cauliflower, and potato curry, which gains pop from a sprinkling of roasted almonds. Here, the sauce has a warm, appealing balance. All you have to do is resist the urge to dredge XYZ's bum naan through it.

And we're back to the naan. Endings don't always have to exactly mirror beginnings, but internal consistency is important: A positive review shouldn't take a starkly negative detour at the halfway point. Conceptually, you should always wind up where you started.

But what about the less cerebral stuff that falls between what your eighth-grade English teacher would have labeled your thesis statement and conclusion? Pulling off a comprehensive – and comprehensible – review which vaults you into online reviewing's highest ranks requires careful planning, a process we'll probe in the next chapter.

CHAPTER 5

How a Critic Approaches a Restaurant

BEFORE I FOUND FULL-TIME WORK as a food critic, I sold wedding dresses. I worked with an incredibly diverse group of brides: It wasn't unusual to spend the morning with a professional cheerleader who wanted something slinky for her beach ceremony and the afternoon with a rural schoolteacher whose highest priority was keeping her upper arms covered. But what all the women had in common was a desire to find the very prettiest dress. Judging from the reactions of their aunts and mothers, for whom we kept boxes of tissues on every available flat surface, they succeeded. Every future bride achieved an individual fashion peak through the right combination of satin, taffeta, and lace.

But what if a bride became so smitten with her dress and the compliments it attracted that she decided to wear it regularly? Would the gown which provoked tears in the chapel play as well at the bowling alley? Obviously not: A dress that's beautiful at a wedding is plum crazy on the weekend. When it comes to clothing, context is everything. Different outfits are designed for different occasions.

Judging from the number of women I saw in bridal gear when I last bowled, I'd venture most folks are keen to the variances of fashion. But a remarkable number of online review writers have trouble translating the notion to restaurants, which are equally divergent. Yelp is riddled with reviews from eaters scandalized by the state of the bathroom in a barbecue joint or brusque service at a banh mi shop. They're hung up on the edible equivalent of a wedding dress, circumstances be damned.

It's hugely important for reviewers to remember that different restaurants serve different purposes. The critic's job is not to judge whether a restaurant meets a predetermined set of criteria for greatness, but *whether it succeeds in doing what it has set out to do.* Olive Garden, for example, is not a great Italian restaurant like Babbo or Marea. But that's not Olive Garden's aim. According to the chain's website, Olive Garden's goal is to "serve fresh, delicious Italian food in a comfortable, home-like setting." Ergo the endless breadsticks. Olive Garden exists to offer affordable, predictable, Italian-inspired dishes to families which don't want to put on airs when they dine out. By that measure, it's A-OK.

If you return to the review of XYZ in the previous chapter, you'll encounter the use of this very yardstick. Only after establishing how the restaurant was positioning itself – "*conspicuously posh lounge*" and "*upscale Indian food*" are among the hints – did I weigh in on its capabilities ("*the restaurant's sloppy cooking is its ultimate undoing*").

The reviewer's first job, then, is to decipher a restaurant's mission. These days, most restaurants don't make a secret of it: If you visit a restaurant's website or listen to what the server says when you respond that you indeed haven't dined with them before, you'll probably have all the information you need. But if the restaurant doesn't broadcast its intentions, there are manifold clues in the dining room.

Start by examining the menu. Are there lots of dishes or just a few? Is everyone eating the very same thing? It's especially common for East Asian restaurants to specialize in just one dish, no matter what the menu lists, although plenty of homegrown restaurants take the same approach. That's why nobody orders a burger at a fish-and-chips stand.

If the restaurant offers a full complement of dishes, pay close attention to their descriptions, whether or not you plan to order them. Do the dishes sound like something a *Top Chef* contestant might serve, signaling trendiness? Or would your grandmother recognize every dish on the menu, suggesting a more traditional bent? Is there a children's or seniors' menu? Does the chef favor seasonings or ingredients associated with a particular cuisine?

Prices can also reveal what kind of crowd the restaurant is hoping to attract: If the menu includes a $5 sandwich section, you're dealing with a restaurant which specializes in quick workday lunches. Alternately, an extensive wine list implies you're meant to linger.

The menu's helpful because it's the primary statement of the restaurant's ambitions. But almost anything within management's control serves the same function. There's not much to be gleaned from a plate of burnt French fries, since it's almost certain botched food wasn't in the business plan. Look instead to the elements which were deliberately chosen to express the restaurant's sensibilities: the art on the walls (or lack thereof); the size and shape of the plates; the background music; the noise level; and the number of seats.

Once you've established the nature of a restaurant, you

can begin to think critically about it. Critically, though, doesn't mean negatively. Too many online review writers apparently believe critics operate like health inspectors, trying to root out every instance of failure (I suspect this is why I'm rarely invited to friends' houses for dinner). It's true that honest reviewers won't ignore a restaurant's faults, but they don't gleefully go looking for them. A review meal is not a gotcha game.

So how does a critic approach a restaurant? Excitedly. I enter every new restaurant expecting to be wowed. Readers who think critics revel in writing bad reviews forget that critics have to eat everything they chronicle. There's absolutely no joy in a subpar meal. The critical mindset requires challenging assumptions, making theoretical connections, and welcoming new experiences. It has nothing to do with pessimism.

Still, keeping an open mind is merely the first step. To assemble a worthy restaurant analysis, a critic has to be an active observer. The following checklist, a version of which exists in every critic's head, is designed to help you generate the meat for a review's all-important middle section:

LOCATION
- Is the building old or new?
- How would you describe the neighborhood?
- What other restaurants are in the vicinity?
- Where's the nearest restaurant specializing in the same cuisine?

DÉCOR
- How is the restaurant lit?
- Does the room have windows?
- Are the chairs comfortable?

- Is the next table at a reasonable distance from yours?
- What's the room's color scheme?
- Can you see the kitchen?
- What's on the walls?
- What's on the table?
- What's the focal point of the room?

AMBIENCE

- How loud is the room? (Smartphone apps for measuring decibel levels abound.)
- What are most diners wearing?
- What are people at nearby tables discussing?
- Is there music playing? (Back to the smartphone if you don't recognize the songs.)
- Are there televisions in the room?
- Can you dine outside?

SERVICE

- Does the restaurant take reservations? If not, how long did you wait for a table?
- Where do guests wait for a table?
- How do staffers address guests?
- Are the staffers neatly dressed?
- What's the pace of service?
- Do staffers speak English?
- Are servers well-versed in the menu?
- What's your server's demeanor?
- Can you always find a server when needed?

MENU

- How many dishes are listed on the menu?
- Do the dishes match up stylistically?
- What's the bravest dish on the menu?

- What's the most popular dish?
- What's housemade? What's not?
- Are the ingredients consistent with the season?
- Which ingredients are repeated most frequently?
- How often does the menu change?
- Is there a dominant cooking style (i.e., frying, sous vide, etc.)?
- What would a vegetarian eat here?
- Is the kitchen willing to adjust dishes?
- Are off-menu specials available?
- Is there a prix-fixe option?
- Is the menu printed in multiple languages?
- Are the menus clean?
- Is there a printed dessert menu?
- If there's a paper menu, take it with you. Otherwise, use your smartphone to photograph it.

BEVERAGES

- Are there non-alcoholic options?
- Does the restaurant use appropriate glassware for its wines, beers, and cocktails?
- Are wines served at the proper temperature?
- Can the server answer questions about the wine list?
- Does the bar serve local spirits, wines, or beers?

FOOD: PREPARATION

- Does the kitchen use any kind of special equipment?
- Are there any aromas emanating from the kitchen?
- Are fish and meats cooked to the requested temperature?
- Does the frying oil taste clean?
- Are sauces and dressings applied in correct proportion?
- Are meats correctly butchered, trimmed, and sliced?

- How meticulously are the vegetables cut?
- Are dishes prepared as described on the menu?
- Are the ingredients fresh?

FOOD: PRESENTATION
- Does the food look appetizing?
- Are the dishes' components arranged artistically?
- Do the dishes feature a range of colors?
- Are the plates and utensils clean?

FOOD: TASTE
- Are the dishes properly seasoned?
- Are the flavors balanced?
- Do any of the dishes require salt, hot sauce, or other enhancer?
- Do the dishes feature a range of textures?
- Does the food taste like anything you've previously eaten?
- Would you order a dish again?

GENERAL
- What is the restaurant most proud of?
- Who's the restaurant's target customer? What would she or he like best about the restaurant?
- How does the restaurant complement or contribute to the local dining scene?

In order to adequately answer the above questions, professional critics strategically structure their review meals. Online reviewers can dispense with the cloak-and-dagger routine which involves reservations and credit cards in fake names. (It has nothing to do with online review writing, but since I'm always asked: The alias credit cards are linked back to an account in a real name. Banks will print cards with whatever name you request, as parents who order credit cards for their children know.) Other methodologies, though, are worth upholding.

I'm a firm believer in showing up hungry, since I don't want to fill up before I've fully explored the menu. Not every critic subscribes to this theory: There are reviewers who think hunger creates bias, because what doesn't taste good when you're starving? While you don't want to fast before a review meal – arriving in a cheerful, optimistic mood is the top priority when critically considering a restaurant – it's not necessary to eat beforehand either. That practice strikes me as silly and costly.

Once seated at a restaurant, your chief concerns are interacting with the service staff and ordering wisely. Professional critics, who have their anonymity to protect and the ability to call back with questions, are sometimes circumspect about quizzing their servers. Online reviewers are free to ask as many questions as they'd like, and ought to exercise the privilege enthusiastically (within reason: If a restaurant's slammed, your server's been triple-sat, and the kitchen smoke alarm just went off, that's probably not the right time to pull a *Portlandia* and ask what kind of chicken laid the eggs for your soufflé). And don't limit your questions to the beginning of the meal: If there's anything nagging you – perhaps you're perplexed by the blueberries on your steak or mystified as to why the bathrooms are co-ed – ask a server or manager to explain. Their responses will help you better understand the restaurant and evaluate whether it's succeeding in doing what it set out to do.

We've already talked about using the menu as a clue to a chef's style and strengths. When it comes to ordering off it, keep those findings in mind. Flexibility is vital. You may have an overwhelming craving for chicken, but if the menu lists eight seafood dishes, filet mignon, and chicken cacciatore, you owe it to the kitchen to try the lobster bisque.

You should always give the restaurant a fair chance to shine. It's ideal to sample an example of each course and cooking style (steaming, frying, roasting, etc.), but if your budget's not compatible with a four-course feast, it's best to resort to the most notorious critic behavior and eat straight off your companions' plates. Far too many online reviews include variations of the phrases "My brother's gyro looked good" and "My wife liked her meatloaf." Grab your fork, friend, and decide for yourself.

•

Eating and writing are intimately related. During a review meal, it's worthwhile to start thinking about what you'll write and how you'll write it. Professional critics certainly do. Assuming you're able to scare up answers to all the questions listed above, as well as to any questions which occur to you at table, you shouldn't have much trouble assembling a review according to a basic template. Although you may eventually opt to depart from the form, it's a more-than-satisfactory starting point.

Section 1: Thesis
You can futz with your lead so it reflects one of the schemes described in the previous chapter, but your main point – the elevator pitch – should be up top. This is where you say, "Tidal Wave is a sushi restaurant for eaters who think cream cheese is too good to use only on bagels" or "Folks who order the creamed corn at Maw-Maw's will never fully appreciate what a chef with three decades of tater-farming

experience can do for mashed potatoes." By the end of this section, readers should know whether or not you liked the restaurant and why.

Section 2: Background
It's not necessary to rewrite the "about us" page of the restaurant's website, but it's a good idea to briefly summarize the restaurant. Remember when you worked out what the restaurant was trying to accomplish? Here's where you insert your conclusion: "Dumpling Dive is the third fried-dumpling counter from a chef who's trying to make vegan fillings palatable to omnivores" or "Joust opened last year to the cheers of nearby college students who've long been starved for Finnish cuisine." You can also use this space to briefly explain your eating resume and relationship to the restaurant: "Roundhouse serves Montreal-style bagels, which I'd never before tried, despite a years-long Sunday-brunching streak."

Section 3: Physical description
No need to get loquacious here. A sentence or two about the restaurant's appearance should suffice.

Section 4: Acknowledgment of other online reviews
As an online reviewer, you're a member of a community, and it's surely courteous to read and comment on what fellow community members have written. You may agree with the prevailing sentiment – "the cinnamon-roll raves are well-deserved" – or politely protest it – "I wouldn't argue with other reviewers' contention that Grub Pub pours a perfect pint, but the bar's myopic focus on beer is sadly reflected in its lackluster wings and jalapeño poppers." And if you're fixing to ream out the restaurant in coming paragraphs, this is an appropriate place to praise the venue for something it does

well: It's a rare restaurant which doesn't have a single thing going for it.

Section 5: Three vignettes underscoring your thesis

Now is the time to talk specifically about food, service, and ambience. You might present one example from each category, or three examples from one category: It's a bit like assembling a gin rummy hand. In any case, what you want to avoid here is the chronological retelling of your restaurant visit. Instead, select three compelling instances which are consistent with your main point.

Say you found a restaurant coldly sterile: That's a prompt to write about the concrete tables, monosyllabic servers, and minimalist poached halibut. Or perhaps you were blown away by the chef's grasp of texture – so write about the snap pea salad, kale chips, and uni cheesecake. If you've done a thorough job of reporting your meal, winnowing your observations to a mere three vignettes may initially feel frustrating. But all your experiences – even those which go unwritten – serve to shape your thesis, which is what's really pivotal.

Section 6: Conclusion

If you've followed the template up to this point, you shouldn't need to introduce any new information here. Tell 'em what you told 'em, and sign off.

You might be worried that applying a template to a creative endeavor will produce a generic object, like an IKEA sofa. But it's very possible to cultivate personality within a set framework. What differentiates a fill-in-the-blank blueprint from an engagingly written review is voice.

CHAPTER 6

Using Your Writer's Voice

VOICE, IN THE WRITERLY SENSE, is sometimes compared to a fingerprint. Whether or not you've been using it, you have a voice and it's utterly unique to you.

The term "voice" is somewhat misleading, since it suggests that the power of your writing correlates with how much style you shoehorn into it. But unlike your speaking or singing voice, you don't amplify your writing voice through force. Your writing voice should be natural, comfortable, and inconspicuous. Once you're practiced at it, your voice will become as instantly recognizable as your body shape, gait, or face.

One way to think about voice is as the humanity behind the words. Voice is what distinguishes your writing from the mechanical text which computers spew; it encompasses the rhythms and word choices that we associate with normal conversation. If you've ever tried to chat with a tech-support operator in a faraway country, you've experienced a lack of voice firsthand.

Voice is intrinsic, meaning it can't be grafted onto your text late in the writing process. You can strengthen your voice in revisions by scrubbing away clichés and axing words you plucked from a thesaurus, but your personality should be apparent from the start.

The best way to avoid muffling your voice is to relax. If you don't write regularly, you may feel pressured to shape your sentences so they sound fancy, or tempted to model your text after other reviews you've read. While it can be instructive to try writing in someone else's voice (How would Hemingway describe this oyster house? What would Toni Morrison say about these crepes Suzette?), it's silly to worry about formal conventions when writing. Just because another online review writer punctuates every sentence with an exclamation point doesn't mean you should follow suit. The very old advice which holds that you should imagine you're writing a letter to a friend is sound. Try writing the way you talk (assuming you don't blather on and on and on). Your prevailing mood – be it thoughtful or antic, skeptical or exuberant – is bound to emerge.

We've already established that voice isn't synonymous with flash. It's also weirdly incompatible with ego. Confident writers don't preface every opinion or observation with an "I." They establish their presence by grounding their writing in their worldviews.

This is hard to follow on the theoretical level, so let's survey a few examples of voice at work. Here, I've paired excerpts from reviews written by leading restaurant critics with excerpts from reviews written by civilian critics. This is entirely unfair: Nobody's going to squander Pulitzer-worthy prose on an online review. As a pedagogical device, it smacks of the

cruelty associated with the monstrous parents who shake
their heads after their kids' cello recitals and cue up a Yo-Yo
Ma track. But it's a decent means of getting at how different
writers express the same thing. After all, who among us hasn't
stared at a tofu scramble and wondered what in the world
hasn't already been said about soy? Let's look at how the pros
go beyond "great" in their own, idiosyncratic voices.

Eating Brussels sprouts at Sparrow, Houston

Yelp review, June 8, 2013

*"The sides we ordered were the Brussels sprouts and potatoes
with crème fraiche. The potatoes tasted great with the steak and
scallops, but it was hard to pay attention to them after one bite
of the Brussels sprouts. THE SPROUTS ARE AMAZING! If you go to
this restaurant and do not order them...I will find you, and I will
judge you for your poor decision. They are just too good to not try
at least once."*

**"Sparrow: Freeing Monica Pope from Her Cage,"
Alison Cook, Houston Chronicle, March 26, 2013**

*[Pope's] seasonal vegetable sides – available singly or as a
satisfying dinner plate of three for $18 – seem more authori-
tative than ever these days. Crisped Brussels sprouts pop with
mustard seeds and red miso. Hearts of baby red cabbage glazed
with tart-sweet balsamic vinegar are soft without, near-meaty
within, fleshed out with caramelized onion and pecans.*

*Roasted baby beets with a beet-green-and-celery pesto taste
like the essence of late Houston spring, right down to the pleas-
antly murky taste of the wilted beet greens alongside. And the
green peas "cacio e pepe" style, like the classic Italian pepper-
and-cheese pasta dish, are tiny miracles of intensity, roughed*

up with aromatic black pepper and then soothed with butter. Who needs noodles when you have peas like these?

Eating English peas at Tar & Roses, Los Angeles

Yelp review, June 11, 2013

"Food and service are great. I tried the oxtail dumpling and it was one of my favorite things on the menu. The wood roasted peas were tasty...minty and salty! The crispy pig tails were yummy. The crisp of the tails and the honey flavor were great. They're a bit messy, so maybe not a first date food, but they're worth trying. I also had the cauliflower which was delicious, and finally the squid fettucini. It was great. If I could have licked my plate I would have."

"A Little Crunch With Your Chianti at Tar & Roses,"
Jonathan Gold, Los Angeles Times, May 5, 2012

If I had to pick the single most delicious thing in the restaurant, it would probably be the English peas, drizzled with oil, sprinkled with sea salt, and roasted until the tough pods collapse into sweetness and the peas inside become smoky little sugar bombs, like edamame as re-imagined in CinemaScope by David Lean. Second might be either the parsnips roasted with crumbled pancetta or that marrow bone, sawed in half and served with the grilled toast called fettunta, a teaspoonful of onion marmalade, and a handful of barely tamed Italian parsley leaves tossed with strands of lemon zest. Is the marrow unevenly cooked? Yes, it is – sometimes it's melted, sometimes still clumpy, but it absorbs the smoke gorgeously.

Assessing the décor at Johnny V's, New Orleans

Urbanspoon review, Sept. 20, 2012

"The décor is awesome! It exudes New Orleans. This place is a must! A great perk is that its attached to an awesome bar. So many beautiful bartenders and excellent service."

"New Orleans Restaurant Johnny V's Earns Three Beans," Brett Anderson, The Times Picayune, June 22, 2012

The much more pressing issue is a dining room that is transporting for all the wrong reasons. The scene Johnny V's appears to be straining to set is a French Quarter courtyard at night. The method is artlessly literal: Stars flicker on the ceiling. Gas lanterns appear between tables and fixed high on the walls alongside fake balconies. The effect brings to mind a Vegas casino's idea of what is lovely about Venice, or a Nativity scene re-created on someone's lawn at Christmas.

The dining room is deaf to the idea that New Orleans' great atmosphere is organic, not manufactured, and it stands in jarring contrast to Hughes' often excellent food, which is rooted in traditions associated with good taste.

Noshing on guacamole at Smack Shack, Minneapolis

TripAdvisor review, May 25, 2013

"On the server's recommendation, we started with the Lobster Guacamole, a flavorful creamy guacamole topped with chunks of lobster – absolutely delicious! Needless to say, we scraped as much as possible out of the dish before letting our server take it

away."

"Triumph of the Lobsters,"
Dara Moskowitz Grumdahl, Mpls.St.Paul, May 2013

The warm smoked duck salad, by head chef Jason Schellin, who made his name at Muffuletta, could have come straight off the menu at that quiet locavore spot: The duck was nicely cooked, and the dried cherries and spiced maple-glazed pecans were a nice, if not particularly groundbreaking, touch. It was an utterly solid salad, and I don't know who goes to a lobster shack for a duck salad, but that person will be happy. A few of the lobster dishes seemed strange. A lobster Cobb salad and the lobster guacamole, for instance, had a desperate sense of: Well, what else can we do with lobster!? What if we put it on a hat? *And since it's lobster, that would probably be a tasty hat.*

Falling in love with Il Buco Alimentari, New York City

Yelp review, June 9, 2013

"How could anyone give this place 1 star? The food is off the charts good. The short ribs are the best we have ever had, not greasy or fatty, like most. We had the Hamachi crudo with an amazing cucumber granite and roe that was the top 10 summer appetizers of all time. Fried artichoke and porchetta with white beans, the whole brazino with grilled lemons, fried polenta, amazing kale; great wines…I could go on and on."

"A Map of Your Tastebuds Shaped Like Italy,"
Pete Wells, The New York Times, Feb. 14, 2012

Is it crazy to fall for a restaurant because of a handful of chickpeas? Tumbling around with pickled currants under crunchy stalks of grilled octopus leg, these chickpeas were smaller and sweeter than usual, less starchy and grainy. Tasting one was like encountering a goldfinch if the only birds you'd ever seen were pigeons.

Still, they were just chickpeas. Is it more logical to fall for a restaurant because of sliced bread in a basket? It was remarkable stuff, with the gradually unfolding nuances of taste that are achieved only through a slow and patient fermentation of dough with wild yeast.

But other restaurants serve great bread. So let's blame it on the salumi board, with satiny pink and white folds of lonza and capocollo and lardo that melt on the tongue into a lasting impression of salt, pig fat, and time. The meats, cured and aged in the basement of Il Buco Alimentari e Vineria, are among the finest salumi in the country.

Our last quoted Yelper raises the contentious issue of stars. Unfortunately, no matter how beautifully you write, many readers are interested only in the bottom line. If you invest time and care in reporting and writing, determining a star rating becomes infinitely easier. But easier isn't easy, which is why we'll next take up the fine art of star assignment.

CHAPTER 7

Assigning Stars

PROFESSIONAL CRITICS WHO ARE REQUIRED to sum up their reviews with stars inevitably get an earful about their rating systems: Many readers struggle to understand why falafel trucks and ritzy French restaurants are eligible for the same numerical designation, or how a generally positive review can be accompanied by two stars.

Every newspaper establishes its own rating criteria, but the Association of Food Journalists' critics guidelines suggest definitions which aren't too far removed from what many publications have adopted:

FOUR STARS: (Extraordinary) Transcendent. A one-of-a-kind experience that sets the local standard.

THREE STARS: (Excellent) Superior. Memorable, high-quality food; exciting environs; savvy service;

smart concept.

TWO STARS: (Good) Solid example of restaurant type.

ONE STAR: (Fair) Just OK. A place not worth rushing back to. But, it might have something worth recommending: A view, a single dish, friendly service, lively scene.

NO STAR: (Poor) Below-average restaurants.

Yelp also uses a five-point system. But the site doesn't ever state what its stars mean, leaving it up to reviewers to decide on their own definitions. That's terrifically problematic, since two reviewers with the same positive opinion of a meal could legitimately come up with wildly different ratings. For example, if a Yelp reviewer adhered to the formula endorsed by the Association of Food Journalists, he or she would give two stars to a restaurant which succeeded in doing what it set out to do. But another Yelp reviewer who'd devised a system in which every restaurant starts with five stars to lose would give the eminently decent restaurant a perfect grade.

There's some evidence that online reviewers are more likely to fall into the latter camp. According to data shared by Yelp, 39 percent of reviews (not just restaurant reviews) are accompanied by five stars. Moving down the ladder, another 27 percent are four-starred, while three-star reviews account for 13 percent of the total. Only 8 percent of reviews feature a two-star rating. The balance belongs to the rarely used one-star rating, appearing with just 13 percent of reviews.

It's a shame that online reviewers aren't more enamored of the three-star review. If I were to compile a simple starring formula for online reviews, I'd suggest awarding three stars to any restaurant to which you'd be willing to return. If you *want* to dine there again, that's a four-star situation. Alternately, if you'd urge your friends to consider dining somewhere else, you're in two-star territory. That's it. No obsessing about the color of the tablecloths or the price of the tapenade: The star rating is a quantitative expression of your gut instinct.

As for the one- and five-star ratings, I'd rarely touch them. A one-star rating, which can prove disastrous for a restaurant, should be reserved for the most outrageous situations: Unless your experience included cockroaches, mouse droppings, raised voices, or stumbling-drunk servers dropping spaghetti in your lap, you've been spared a one-star restaurant. (I'd hesitate to put food poisoning on the list of outrages, since it's typically difficult to determine with certainty whether a restaurant was responsible for making you sick, which nudges the allegation into the potentially libelous realm. In many, if not most, cases of foodborne illness, the pathogen was picked up at home. Remember, too, that no commercial kitchen is above food-safety concerns: Copenhagen's Noma, named "best restaurant in the world" for three years running, poisoned 70 diners in March 2013.)

A five-star restaurant is like pornography: You'll know it when you see it, and it will likely bring you great pleasure. To earn five stars, a restaurant should serve up an experience you'll remember all your dining days.

The foregoing notwithstanding, so long as the Yelp rating system is broken – Harvard Business School professor Michael Luca has proposed a model in which reviews would be run through an algorithm which accounts for reviewers' track records and quality changes over time, but he says Yelp's not biting – a little grade inflation may be in order. If you want to bump up your rating by one star to better reflect the realities of online reviewing, I promise I won't fuss about it. After all, opinions are better conveyed through prose than points, as the superior reviews in the next chapter prove.

CHAPTER 8

Reviews That Work

DESPITE ALL THE DIVERSITY IN restaurants and the reviews written about them, we've now zeroed in on a few shared qualities of fair, useful, and readable reviews. Whether published online or in print, the best reviews are grounded in thorough reporting, open-mindedness, and an understanding of restaurant operations; they're elevated by the following attributes:

- Defined perspective
- Defensible opinion
- Holistic approach (which entails thinking beyond oneself)
- Attention to detail
- Multisensory descriptions
- Quantitative references
- Clear, coherent, and concise writing

- Voice

So what happens when all that's rustled up in service of a taco stand? Here are a few real Yelp reviews which demonstrate how it's done.

The Sycamore, San Francisco
>   **Writer:** Leslie P.
>   **Date:** 12/13/12
>   **Highlights:**
>>   - *Defined perspective*
>>   - *Defensible opinion*
>>   - *Attention to detail*

What a fun brunch with great food – and the bottomless mimosas are not to be ignored, either. In fact, the mimosa server was the most popular person in the whole joint, never letting anyone's glass run dry, and the orange juice they used was fantastic – perfectly pulpy, with a great ratio of juice to sparkle.

We had a variety of food: one each of the sliders, pork belly donuts, chicken and waffles, and more. I focused on the chicken and waffles and the pork belly donuts. Chicken and waffles are not usually my thing, but these were so delicious. The chicken was a bit overcooked, but the waffles made the dish – stuffed with manchego cheese and prosciutto with a Maker's Mark and maple syrup, topped with kiwi – so good. It was hard to move on to the pork belly donuts.

Once I tried the donuts, though, all bets were off. They were the perfect balance of salt, savory, and sweet with more of the Maker's Mark glaze to top it all off. I could have eaten at least another order if not more.

It was interesting to watch people get frustrated with the order system. It says clear as day at the top of the menu that you order from the bartender, then someone brings out your food. However, quite a few people left in a huff assuming the service was poor without even bothering to look at the menu to see the instructions.

   With a patio and indoor seating, bottomless mimosas and inventive food, this place fills up quick. Prepare to wait, but definitely go, and definitely grab a board game off the shelf to play with your friends or people sitting nearby!"

Prosperity Dumpling, New York City
Writer: Paul V.
Date: 5/6/13
Highlights:
- *Holistic approach*
- *Quantitative references*
- *Voice*

Good. Cheap. Dumplings. What more could you ask for?
How was the service and atmosphere?
As has been well-documented thus far, Prosperity embodies all that is classic New York grit and grind. It's cramped, it's dingy, and the weather indoors matches that outside thanks to the door always being open. Service is no-nonsense, and if you don't know what you want? Get out of line rookie. However, be rest assured friends, you'll get your order quickly, and it'll be correct.
How were the portions relative to the cost?
Hold on to your hats folks. See these 10 fried dumplings? Well, those dumplings (all ten of them) are going to cost you $2.75. Yes, you heard that right. Ten dumplings. $2.75. That's it. That's all. The end. It's quite possibly the best price to portion ratio I've ever seen.
How was the food?

$2.75. For ten. I want you to keep that in mind folks, because while you often get what you pay for? Here at Prosperity? Well, you get slightly more than you pay for.

As you might guess, these aren't the best dumplings in the world (even if you can get your hands on boiled instead of fried, which is a rarity) Having said that? They have all the essentials, and particularly if you're in a less-than-sober state? You're going to absolutely love them. I'll be honest, I didn't feel amazing afterwords, but I didn't have any regrets.

Would you eat here every day if you could?

With so many other options? No, but PD is worth a stop if you're in the city.

Teardrop Cocktail Lounge, Portland, Ore.
Writer: Valery C.
Date: 1/2/13
Highlights:
- *Multisensory descriptions*
- *Clear, coherent, and concise writing*

In this coolly refined lounge of stone and glass, the focal point is the polished teardrop-shaped bar. Teardrop is well-regarded in Portland's cocktail scene, and on this early afternoon as sunlight streamed into the elegant room, I felt immediately at home, taking in the sights of a well-kept bar, from fresh citrus and juices to herbs to the long row of bright blue dropper bottles of housemade bitters and tinctures. Spirits hung above the center, in its own teardrop-shaped clear tray. The bartenders are dapper in their vests and suspenders, and professional.

The cocktail menu, updated seasonally, was rewardingly long, a page each of house creations, old classics (or twists of), and creations plucked from bars around the country. I suppose I could happily read their menu several times over and not lose interest; the creations are fascinating, inspired, and frankly exciting. They helpfully include a glossary of terms to help decipher many of the modifiers used, of which there seems to be an endless number.

Having taken a fancy to Cocchi Americano as well as looking for ways to use my own bottle of Scrappy's grapefruit bitters, I found both in their Lindberg's Baby, a recipe from Cook & Brown Public House in Rhode Island. Added to a base of Ransom Old Tom gin, with apricot-flavored Marie Brizard Apry and Bitter Truth Jerry Thomas bitters, this was a wickedly good cocktail well balanced by the bitters and fruit aromas, no easy feat with the range of ingredients at play.

Beyond cocktails, a tequila flight in the classic set of a blanco, reposado, and anejo surprised with some wonderful housemade sangritas. I don't recall the ingredients that our bartender named, but there was tomato water and roasted tomatillo. The sangritas were delicious enough to stand on their own, but served to elevate the flight.

A sublime cocktail lounge of remarkable craftsmanship. There's table seating including some limited outdoor seating, but while this would be an upscale lounge experience, for me the show is at the bar and for that, I'd come alone or with just one or two others to enjoy the artistry.

CHAPTER 9

Practice Exercises

THE VERY BEST WAY TO improve your reviewing skills is to eat, write, and repeat. But targeted exercises can be helpful if you're looking to work on a particular aspect of your reviewing practice.

To eradicate clichés: Print out half a dozen reviews from professional critics you admire. Underline every instance of a phrase which is the creative equivalent of one of the following popular online phrases:

- "It was great."
- "It looked good."
- "The dish was too sweet."
- "The dish was flavorless."
- "The dish was huge."

To better appreciate the power of voice: Print two unformatted reviews apiece from half a dozen professional critics. Try to pair the reviews written by the same author.

To enhance descriptive skills, Part I: Prepare a plate of dinner. Write 20 sentences describing the food, none of which reference taste.

To enhance descriptive skills, Part II: Recall the best meal you've had in the past year. Write a 350-word description of the food without using the words "delicious," "amazing," "incredible," "wonderful," or "yummy."

To broaden your perspective: Recall the worst meal you've had in the past year. Write a short review from the perspective of a diner who loved it.

CHAPTER 10

Putting It All Together

GENERALLY, THE GOAL OF A how-to book is to put a new skill within easy reach of the reader. With the right book, non-artists can learn to paint convincing watercolors of tulips and non-musicians can learn to play the ukulele. This book's taken a slightly different tack, arguing that a goodly number of folks who are already writing online reviews haven't yet mastered the medium. Restaurant criticism is harder than it seems.

Still, with the right tools, amateur critics can produce solid reviews which have far greater value to society than another picture of pretty flowers. Having read this book, those tools now belong to you. To see what you can do with them, let's reconvene with Debbie and Denise, the diners we met at The Standard way back in Chapter 1. If you're still in a participatory mood after the recent round of practice exercises, you might want to try writing an online review based on their meal. If not, have a gander at Denise's write-up, which conveniently reflects all the principles we've discussed:

> With its wide-ranging menu of American comfort foods and overstuffed banquette seating, The Standard seems designed to appeal to everyone. But the restaurant is sometimes careless with the customers it's already attracted.
>
> The Standard opened last year, replacing a mediocre pizzeria which nobody misses, me included – and I'm partial to anything with melted cheese. Still, when my friend told me a trusted farmers-market vendor was a fan of the chef, I was happy to go the healthy route for once.
>
> The centerpiece of The Standard is an open kitchen, although the warm lighting in the dining room is so flattering that I'd wager most coupled diners don't take their eyes off each other. Since we hadn't made a reservation, it took 40 minutes before we were granted access to the dining room. We whiled away the time in the cozy bar. The Standard serves cocktails, beer, and wine, although possibly not enough of the latter: My friend's vinho verde was oxidized. Yet as other reviewers have written, the bartenders are extraordinarily attentive. A bartender replaced the wine without complaint, providing the evening's standout service.
>
> Once we were seated, the restaurant's professionalism appeared to flag. We weren't alerted to the overwhelming heat of a grilled-prawn starter, featuring fat shrimp dunked in a peppery tomato sauce flecked with feta. Forgetfulness also spoiled my friend's steak salad, which was served with dressing despite her request for dressing on the side. And we again felt as though the restaurant hadn't made its guests its top priority when we learned carrot cake was the only dessert still available at 8 p.m.
>
> I would return to The Standard for its tart mojito and roast-

ed chicken, a wonder of juicy meat and golden, crisped skin. The neatly trimmed New York strip aboard the admirably green salad was also beautifully cooked. But I genuinely hope the young restaurant sorts out its distracting service issues.

That's it. Now it's your turn. Good luck.

Questions? I'd love to hear from you. E-mail me at greatonlinerestaurantreviews@gmail.com. Or visit with me on Twitter at @hannaraskin.

Acknowledgments

TRUE TO THE SPIRIT OF online restaurant reviewing, this book benefitted enormously from the contributions of many talented and passionate people who were unreasonably generous with their time and expertise.

Many thanks to Alan Brown, whose dedication to Yelping well inspired the idea for a how-to guide, and Rebekah Denn, who first said the magic letter "e" when I floated my grand scheme.

I'm also indebted to copy editor Gavin Borchert, for double-checking every dot and dash, CL Smith, for noodling with the cover, and readers Deb Brown and Emily Miller, for their valuable perspective.

It's testament to Matthew Amster-Burton's services that you wouldn't be able to read these words if he hadn't taught me how to format them correctly. Matthew was the Old Toby along my trail of discovery, cluing me into every necessary step in the self-publishing process. This book wouldn't exist without him.

And finally, my deepest gratitude belongs to my husband, Kenny, who supported this project from the start. His unwavering enthusiasm and incredible tolerance for my extended writing sessions and wrenching typeface dilemmas made this book possible. Five stars.

About the Author

Hanna Raskin is the food writer for the Charleston, S.C. Post & Courier. She previously served as food critic for the Seattle Weekly and Dallas Observer, earning recognition from the James Beard Foundation, Association of Alternative Newsmedia and the Association of Food Journalists for her work. A founding member of Foodways Texas and an active member of the Southern Foodways Alliance, Raskin serves on the board of the Association of Food Journalists. Her writing has appeared in Modern Farmer, Journal of Popular Culture, Cooking Light, Southern Living and Garden & Gun.

3862673R00059

Made in the USA
San Bernardino, CA
23 August 2013